Lily F. Wesselhoeft

The Fairy-Folk of Blue Hill

Lily F. Wesselhoeft

The Fairy-Folk of Blue Hill

ISBN/EAN: 9783743382800

Manufactured in Europe, USA, Canada, Australia, Japa

Cover: Foto ©ninafisch / pixelio.de

Manufactured and distributed by brebook publishing software (www.brebook.com)

Lily F. Wesselhoeft

The Fairy-Folk of Blue Hill

The Fairy-Folk of Blue Hill

BY

LILY F. WESSELHOEFT

Author of "Sparrow the Tramp," Etc.

ILLUSTRATED

BOSTON
JOSEPH KNIGHT COMPANY
1895

COPYRIGHT, 1894
BY
JOSEPH KNIGHT COMPANY

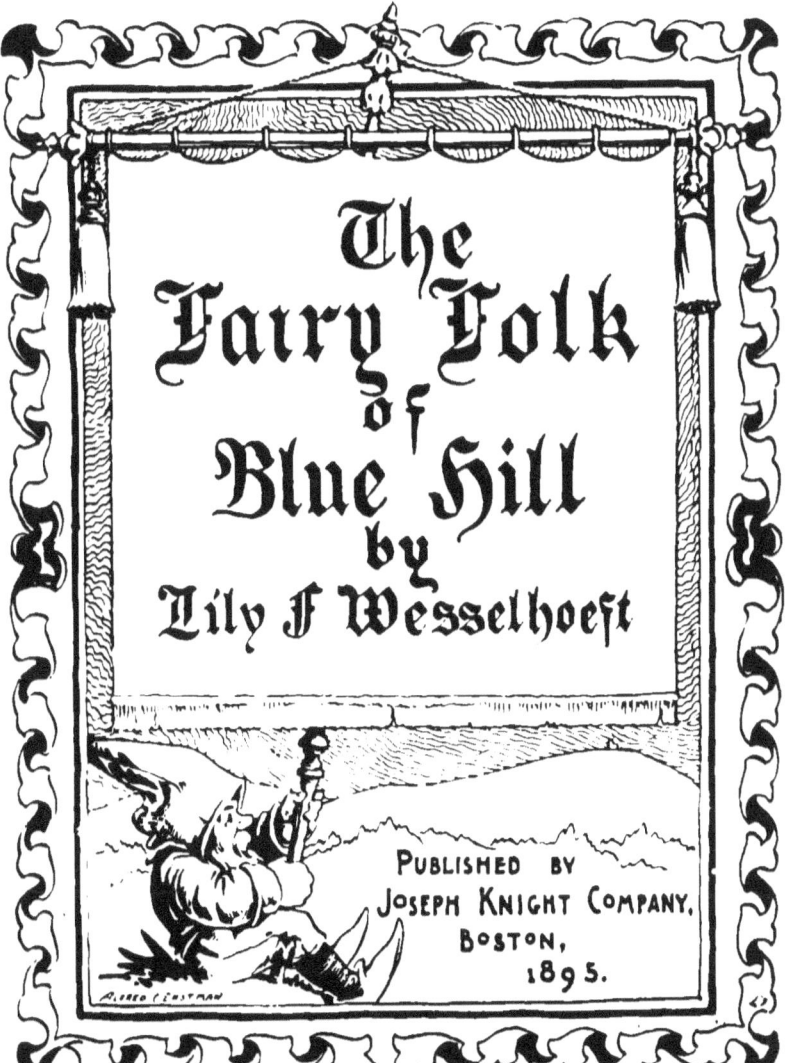

The Fairy Folk of Blue Hill

by Lily F Wesselhoeft

PUBLISHED BY
JOSEPH KNIGHT COMPANY,
BOSTON,
1895.

CONTENTS

CHAP.		PAGE
I.	THE MISCHIEVOUS PRANK OF THE GNOMES	1
II.	WHAT THE BROWN BEETLE SAW	14
III.	WASSA'S THEFT	28
IV.	FAIRY WELL AND PLOT OF GNOMES	42
V.	WASSA MAKES A PLAN	58
VI.	THE ELVES AND GNOMES TO THE RESCUE	74
VII.	FAIRYLAND	84
VIII.	WASSA GOES TO FAIRYLAND	99
IX.	THE BROWN BEETLE UNDERTAKES A MISSION	114
X.	THE LAND OF THE AFTER-GLOW	128
XI.	WASSA RETURNS TO FAIRYLAND	143
XII.	THE FAIRY PRINCE AND THE MERMAIDS	157
XIII.	WASSA GOES TO THE LAND OF THE MID-DAY MOON AND FINDS THE FAIRY PRINCE	171
XIV.	THE FAIRY PRINCE AND WASSA	183
XV.	WASSA CAPTURES THE FAIRY PRINCE	198
XVI.	CLOUDCATCHER AND HIS PRISONERS	214
XVII.	THE LITTLE GRAY MAN'S DECISION	225

List of Illustrations

	PAGE
The departure of the giants . . . . Frontispiece.	
Illuminated Title	vii
Headpiece to Table of Contents	ix
Tailpiece to Table of Contents	ix
Headpiece to List of Illustrations	xi
Tailpiece to List of Illustrations	xiii
Headpiece to Chapter I	1
"They silently gathered about the sleeping giant cook" . .	6
"As in their midst stood a little gray man"	10
"Up the steep hill the gnomes toiled"	16
"A beautiful blue dragon-fly alighted on a stone near by" .	18
Tailpiece to Chapter II	27
"Her parents had recently built a hut on the shore of Lily Pond"	33
"Wassa skilfully extricated the fishes"	35
Tailpiece to Chapter III	41
"It was little Mona, the hunter's child"	45
"Toto the Slim was seen astride the limb of an oak" . . .	50
"As the song ceased, the gnomes paused in their work" . .	55
"The two giants who were to carry away the hut cautiously approached	61

xii   LIST OF ILLUSTRATIONS.

	PAGE
"Mona's light cap fell off"	70
"Carefully she caught the boughs that came in her way"	72
Tailpiece to Chapter V	73
Headpiece to Chapter VI	74
"Others blew long blasts"	77
"At a table . . . sat King Rondo"	81
Headpiece to Chapter VII	84
"The gnomes, at the bidding of King Rondo, gently lifted the hunter's little maid"	85
"My dear, where hast thou been so long?"	89
"I came to see the beautiful things that Mona, the hunter's maid told me about"	102
"The little maid bent forward and gazed eagerly into the turbid water"	104
"A large bird with a hideous face and long bill flew close to her"	106
Headpiece to Chapter IX	114
"Help! screamed Wassa, striving vainly to extricate herself"	123
Tailpiece to Chapter IX	127
"Gradually the column of mist assumed the form of a beautiful female figure"	129
"In a crotch of the huge tree was Judge Owl"	132
"Rockroller approached the mass of rock"	139
Tailpiece to Chapter X	142
"He amused himself by reaching far over the edge of the pond"	151
"After a tedious walk, the cave of the birds was reached"	152
"The delicate form of a fairy appeared within"	155
Tailpiece to Chapter XI	156
"A fairy boat that sailed rapidly toward the prince and Wassa"	159

LIST OF ILLUSTRATIONS.

	PAGE
"The monarch of the sea"	162
"So engaged in watching the mermaids was Wassa"	167
Headpiece to Chapter XIII	171
"She beheld a beautiful palace of the purest crystal"	173
"She sprang joyfully forward to seize a luscious plum"	177
"The Prince and Wassa seated themselves on the beautiful creature's back"	188
"The eagle spread his long wings and soared into the sky"	190
"The dark head of a rattlesnake came into view"	196
Tailpiece to Chapter XIV	197
"She constantly reared her head to gaze into the kettle"	200
"A light form stood before her"	206
"Wassa looked up, and saw, over the top of the huge rock, the head of a giant"	210
"King Cloudcatcher, holding his hood in his hand"	215
"A merry twinkle came into the king's bright eyes"	221
Tailpiece to Chapter XVI	224
"And placing the elf on the top of it"	226
"The giant Twigtwister"	234
Tailpiece to Chapter XVII	240

THE FAIRY-FOLK OF THE BLUE HILL.

CHAPTER I.

The Mischievous Prank of the Gnomes.

Hundreds and hundreds of years ago, dear children, there lived on the beautiful Blue Hill a family of giants.

Peaceable fellows, in the main, were these giants, usually living in harmony with one another, although deep mutterings were occasionally heard to issue from the neighborhood of the hill; these sometimes grew so loud that they shook the earth, and then the timid rabbits scurried into their holes, and the sensitive birds hastened to hide themselves in the depths of the wood, thinking a thunder storm was coming.

The brown beetle, however, knew better. *He* knew, when he heard these sounds, that the giants were quarrelling. He had seen the little man in gray, who always appeared when the quarrels became violent, and the brown beetle knew well the power this little man possessed over the great blustering fellows,— he knew how quickly all disputes ceased when the little figure, clad in gray, appeared in their midst.

The brown beetle knew well this little gray man, whom the timid rabbits and birds thought to be but a streak of mist. Oh! the brown beetle could have told them many a tale, if they would but have listened to him! It is not to be wondered at, that they thought the little gray man but a streak of mist, for they were too much frightened to take a good look at him.

The brown beetle, though of dull mind, understood fully the power of the little gray man over the great and powerful giants with their childish minds. He knew, although his slow brain could not have expressed it in words, that the great, childish fellows felt the power of the stronger mind of the little man in gray, who controlled their natures, since they could not do it themselves.

As we said before, the giants were usually good-natured, and if they did no great good, certainly did no great harm. They amused themselves by striding about the country, reaching the neighboring towns in half a dozen good strides,— fishing in the surrounding ponds, and basking in the sunlight that lay on the sides of the Blue Hill.

The quarrels among the giants seldom amounted to more than a few high words that were soon forgotten, as is the case of brothers and sisters of the human family; but these giants had enemies, and, strange to say, these enemies, the only ones they feared, were the very opposite of themselves, as small as they were large, and were no other than the small gnomes or dwarfs who lived in underground caves and beneath large stones.

It would seem as if the great giants might

have taken care of themselves, but strange as it may seem, they were no match for the wary little dwarfs, who, having ten times more brains in their little heads than the giants had in their great empty noddles, drove the giants almost to distraction by their impish and ingenious tricks.

Early one morning, the giants departed for a day's tramp. From the summit of Blue Hill, on clear days, they could see the snowy peaks of the mountain now known as Mt. Washington, and they were curious to know if it were as large as their own Blue Hill, for it looked very small in the distance. So off they set, leaving behind one of their number, with instructions to have plenty of hot oatmeal porridge for them on their return, for a hundred miles was quite a little walk for them, and they knew that the exercise would give them an appetite.

As soon as the giants were gone, the cook stepped over to the next town and collected dry sticks suitable for his fire, piling them up in a great heap, all ready to be lighted. Then, as it was a warm day, and it would not be necessary for him to cook his porridge for some time, he lay down in the shade and dreamed away the afternoon.

As the sun slowly settled into the western woods, the giant remembered that it was time for him to begin his cooking, so he rubbed two smooth sticks briskly together until a spark appeared, and in a minute more the smoke curled up over the trees, and the oatmeal porridge was bubbling away merrily.

It is not very exciting work making oatmeal porridge, and the fire was quite hot, too, for it required a very large pot to hold enough porridge for all the giants, and consequently a large fire was needed, a fire, in fact, as large as the great Boston fire of 1872. So the giant thought he might as well make himself comfortable and seated himself with his back resting against Blue Hill, and his feet comfortably immersed in the cool waters of "Lily Pond." Seated thus, the soothing effect of the foot-bath, together with the crackling of the fire and the bubbling of the porridge, brought about a sleepy condition of the giant cook's great brain, and without knowing it, he fell fast asleep.

No sooner were the giant's eyes closed, than from behind every bush and tree sprang hundreds of little creatures with sturdy forms, long, peaked beards, and comical little caps that ended in a peak. Their faces were brimful of mischief, and they silently gathered

about the sleeping giant cook. After watching the sleeper for a while, and laughing at the foolish expression of his face, as he sat with his great head nodding forward, the king of the gnomes, Rondo by name (and a rosy, good-natured looking monarch he was, who loved good cheer and mischief), jumped upon a stone in the midst of his subjects, and thus addressed them:—

> "Come, subjects mine, the hours are few
> Before the giants home are due.
> Pity 'twould be, now would it not,
> Should they not find the porridge hot?
> Better to find it burnt, I hold,
> Than flavorless, uncooked and cold.
> Then quickly bring me, I desire,
> More fuel for this waning fire."

Then the gnome king jumped down from the stone and went up to the fire that was not waning at all, but doing very well,— in fact, just the right amount of heat to cook the porridge slowly and safely. The other gnomes, meanwhile, were collecting dried sticks and soon returned, laden with bundles of them which they thrust into the fire, King Rondo, at the same time, stirring them with his golden sceptre, in order to create a better draught.

In a few moments, the huge fire was blazing finely, and a great volume of steam arose from the kettle in which the oatmeal porridge was bubbling away furiously. It rose higher and higher in the great kettle, and soon came pouring over the sides and fell into the ashes and fire below. At this, the gnomes laughed with glee and danced about exultantly, King Rondo, all the time, stirring the fire with his golden sceptre.

By this time, the giant cook's slumber became lighter, and he began to move about restlessly in his sleep, as many sound sleepers do when about to wake. He gave such a sudden yawn that the dwarf king jumped back from the fire in haste, and his subjects ran off with great speed.

The giant opened his eyes at the moment when the peaked cap of the dwarf king was disappearing behind a clump of bushes, and he started up with a presentiment that something was wrong, for the dwarfs' visits never boded good to the giants.

At once, the giant's eyes fell on the kettle with the porridge running over its sides, and he became sensible of a decidedly burnt odor. With much trepidation, the giant caught up a large stick, in fact, it was the trunk of a large pine-tree, and scattered the blazing embers from under the kettle. Then he seized the huge spoon and hastily scooped up as much of the porridge as he could, not realizing that he was taking also a large amount of ashes. Not until he had dipped up all the mixture, did he see that the porridge in the kettle was full of black specks. It was too late to remedy the mistake by making fresh porridge, so he resolved to trust to luck and the good appetites of the giants.

Not long did the suspense of the giant cook last, for very soon he recognized the distant voices of his returning friends, and a great panic seized him, as he heard them clamoring for their supper. Putting on as unconcerned a manner as he was able, the cook placed before his hungry companions the hot oatmeal porridge, and awaited, in breathless suspense, the result of the first taste.

"Faugh!" exclaimed one, "the knave has burnt it!" and taking up a spoonful of the mixture, he hurled it far away.

"The stuff is full of ashes," cried another, and he also threw away the contents of his big spoon.

At this, a general hubbub arose, in the midst of which one of the giants seized the huge caldron and hurled the contents far and wide. It fell in the neighboring towns, and, as the giant's rage increased, farther and farther did he hurl the oatmeal, and a huge lump fell in the town we now call Quincy. Then came a still more violent swing of the giant's arm, and a quantity of the porridge was hurled where the town of Gloucester now stands.

On the unfortunate cook fell the brunt of the giants' displeasure, but as their ill-humor increased, a general fight arose, and each giant attacked his neighbor indiscriminately. During the tumult, the cook vainly attempted to make his voice heard and relate how the dwarfs had brought about the mishap, but the giants, unreasonable as angry children, were too excited to listen to him.

The tumult was at its height, the air resounding with the noise of heavy blows and fierce imprecations, when suddenly a silence fell on the savage group, as in their midst stood a little gray man. Gray clothes, hat, beard and hair he had, and the tall giants towered far above him, but every one of them hung his head before the stern gaze of the little man in gray.

"Shame on ye!" exclaimed the little gray man severely, "again have ye broken the contract and disturbed the peace."

It was astonishing to note the change that took place in the countenances of the giants as the little gray man spoke. A moment before raging with the fury of wild beasts, they had suddenly become abject and humble, not daring to raise their downcast eyes before the stern gaze of the little man in gray.

"Pardon, master!" cried one of the giants, his great trembling voice sounding like rumbling thunder. "Pardon, master, we were sorely tried."

A contemptuous smile flitted o'er the lips of the little gray man, as he replied:

"Are ye a parcel of babies that ye must need squabble over a mess of burnt porridge? I would that your great empty heads contained but a small part of the brains my little gnomes possess!"

"Master," said the cook humbly, "they will

not listen to one. The dwarfs it was who burnt the porridge by building a hot fire under it, while I slept."

"It serves thee right, thou great sleepy head," replied the little gray man. "Hadst thou been attending to thy duty as thou shouldst have done, the dwarfs would not have played the trick on thee. Now, listen to your sentence, ye great over-grown children! The next time ye so forget yourselves, shall ye forfeit the right to these pleasant regions and be banished to far-off realms. And now, the fruits of your senseless rage shall ye ever see before ye, to serve ye as a reminder. Hundreds of years hence, when it is forgotten that such a race as ye ever existed, men shall prize a stone that they little dream was once the oatmeal porridge of the giants. Thus shall good come out of your senseless bickerings. Remember my words, and know that I will keep my vow."

Bowing submissively, the giants silently trooped down the hill. The little gray man watched them until, with a few strides, they were out of sight, when his severe countenance relaxed and an amused expression stole over his face, as one sometimes smiles at the recollection of the misdemeanors of children, to whom he has administered a deserved rebuke. Then, as suddenly as he had appeared, the little gray man was gone. How or where, no one could have told, he simply was gone.

The threat of the little gray man was fulfilled. The burnt oatmeal porridge with the specks of cinders in it was congealed where it fell, and to this day, the quarries of Quincy and the Cape Ann Quarry of Gloucester produce handsome blocks of granite, that very few people know was once the burnt oatmeal porridge of the Blue Hill giants.

CHAPTER II.

WHAT THE BROWN BEETLE SAW.

The little brown beetle, seated under a leaf, had seen the mischievous gnomes at work and had heard the quarrel of the giants, and when he saw them so dejected at the reproof of the little man in gray, he felt very sorry for them, for they had never done him any harm, and he had seen so much of them that he felt quite well acquainted with them, and was sure that they were not bad at heart.

The brown beetle thought the little gray man had been unnecessarily severe with the giants, and he trembled as he thought how soon the foolish fellows might do the same thing over again, and how lonesome it would be not to see their great forms moving about, nor to hear the hill reverberating with the echo of their deep voices, nor the crackling of the underbrush beneath their huge feet.

Very depressing was the mood these thoughts

produced, but the brown beetle gradually became more cheerful, and before long he was himself again. Sitting basking on a dry leaf on which the sun was shining, the beetle pondered over the annoyances the mischievous gnomes constantly inflicted on his friends, the giants. Suddenly, he heard a slight crackling of dry branches and leaves that he knew must be caused by the feet of either human beings or animals, which, he could not tell. Anxiously straining his eyes in the direction of the sounds, in a moment there appeared, around the bend in the path, the little man in gray.

Not from the footsteps of the little gray man did the crackling sounds proceed,— never a twig or leaf bent under his light tread. As he came into view around the bend of the path, he turned and, looking back over the steep road over which he had just come, beckoned authoritatively with his hand.

Then to the astonished gaze of the brown beetle, appeared a troop of gnomes, each bearing on his sturdy shoulders a pack. On they came, in single file, by the thousand it seemed to the bewildered beetle, each one an exact counterpart of the other, and each small figure bending beneath the weight of his heavy burden.

Up the steep hill, the gnomes toiled after the little man in gray, and when the last one had

passed, the brown beetle recovered his scattered senses, and curiosity getting the better of his amazement, he spread his wings and flew after them.

When the little man in gray reached the top of the hill, he paused for an instant before a high rocky wall, and, looking over his band of gnomes, addressed them in serious tones:—

"Since ye must needs play your mischievous pranks on the giants, I have decided to confine ye to the interior of this hill, where ye will be safe from the wrath of the enemy. I command ye to keep to the occupation of extending your underground domains, and to cease to annoy my giant subjects, who are dangerous fellows when aroused. Do ye note my commands?"

"We hear and obey, master," replied the gnomes, bowing submissively.

Signing to the band to follow him, at a given signal from the little gray man, the wall of rock parted, and he disappeared within the dark cavern, followed by his obedient subjects. When the last gnome had vanished from sight, the rock rolled back into place, and the brown beetle found himself alone before the closed entrance to the cavern.

"Can I have been dreaming?" said the brown beetle to himself, as he passed one of his prickly feet across his eyes to clear his vision. No; he had not dreamed at all, for there was the cave with its rocky barrier before him, and placing his ear against the rocky door, a confused murmur of tiny voices reached him, and, ere long, the sharp and regular click of two hard substances struck together was heard.

The brown beetle wondered if the gnomes would always remain in their underground home as the little man in gray had commanded them to do, or whether they would roam over the country as they had done, and as the giants did. While

these thoughts were passing through the beetle's mind, a swift whirring of wings attracted his attention, and a beautiful blue dragon-fly alighted on a stone near by.

The blue dragon-fly had a haughty manner, and was attended by a swarm of gnats, whose business it was to wait on her and obey her slightest whim. Not deigning to notice the brown beetle who was gazing admiringly at her, the blue dragon-fly busied herself in arranging her toilet, that was in some disorder from her long flight. She fluttered her gauzy wings and spread them in the sun, all the time apparently unconscious of the presence of the brown beetle, who was admiring, with all his might, the beautiful blue of her graceful body, and the delicacy of her gauzy wings.

Giving the finishing touches to her toilet, the blue dragon-fly threw back her head proudly, and addressed her attendants thus:

"I desire ye to keep further off. Your presence oppresses me."

The gnats obediently withdrew to a short distance, and hovered together in the warm air, while the blue dragon-fly balanced herself gracefully on a stone and, for the first time, looked at the brown beetle.

The beetle was so embarrassed, when the dragon-fly fixed her beautiful great eyes on him, that he hardly knew what he said, but he stammered some words to the effect that he was glad to see her.

"It is a matter of indifference to me," replied the blue dragon-fly haughtily, "whether thou art glad or sorry to see me."

The brown beetle was dreadfully confused at this rude repulse, and hastened to apologize.

"I come and go as I please," continued the proud beauty, "and ask leave of no one. Straighten out the tip of my left wing," she ordered, turning to her attendants.

The submissive waiting-maids hastened to do their queen's bidding, and then in obedience to a sign from her, retired to a distance as before.

"What is the matter with the giants?" demanded the blue dragon-fly imperiously, not deigning to look at the beetle as she addressed him.

The brown beetle, delighted to oblige such a beautiful being, hastened to tell the story of the mischievous trick of the gnomes and the quarrel of the giants, and how the little man in gray had commanded the gnomes to abide in the interior of the hill in future.

The blue dragon-fly beckoned to her attendants to approach.

"Go into yonder cavern and ascertain how the gnomes are employed, and what the cavern is like," ordered the proud queen.

The swarm of gnats obediently flew off to execute the bidding of their mistress, and were soon out of sight. In a short time, they came swarming back again.

"Well?" demanded the queen haughtily.

"We have been able to discover nothing, gracious lady," answered the first maid of honor. "We found our passage barred by a high wall of solid rock, and although a faint murmur of voices reached our ears, we were not able to catch the words."

"Stupid things!" exclaimed the dragon-fly. "Now go and prepare a bath for me."

Away swarmed the eager attendants, and the blue dragon-fly and the brown beetle were left alone together.

The blue dragon-fly looked at the brown beetle quite graciously. "I don't like the dark," she said with a charming smile. "I like to fly about in the sunlight. I suppose that cavern is as dark as dark as can be."

"Oh! yes," replied the beetle, delighted to be addressed by the beautiful stranger, "it's as dark as a pocket. I've often been in there, or rather, a short distance in."

"Thou?" asked the dragon-fly in astonishment. "How was it possible for thee, with thy great clumsy body to enter, when my little gnats, with their tiny forms, found no crevice through which to creep?"

"Low down on the ground, in one corner," replied the beetle, "there is a place where the stone has crumbled away, and there I entered."

"I would go in, but I *do* so hate dark, poky places," said the blue dragon-fly, with a coquettish flutter of her gauzy wings.

"I should think thou wouldst," replied the brown beetle, with a glance of admiration at the pretty creature balancing herself in the air. "Such beautiful beings as thou ought to live in the sunlight."

"Great stupid thing! Why cannot he understand what I want?" muttered the blue dragon-fly, in a low tone; but she took care that her words should not be heard by the brown beetle. "Thou wouldst not mind going in for me, wouldst thou?" she said aloud, with a charming smile.

Mind going in? Not the brown beetle! Why, he would have gone in at the blue dragon-fly's bidding, if he had been sure that some huge creature stood within to gobble him up at the first step he took.

So the brown beetle disappeared through the hole in one corner of the rocky wall, and the dragon-fly, flippant creature that she was, sported in the sunlight, flirting her delicate wings, and skimming about, with no regret at having used her arts to persuade the honest brown beetle to gratify her idle curiosity.

Some minutes passed, and the dragon-fly was becoming impatient at the delay, when the brown beetle reappeared.

"The gnats were right," he said, "there is a second wall of thick stone, behind which it is impossible to go, and where the gnomes are at work."

"Is that all thou hast discovered?" demanded the blue dragon-fly in a disappointed tone. "It appears that the gnats were not the only stupid ones."

The brown beetle took no notice of the rudeness of this remark, but went on with his story:

"Creeping as closely to the wall as I could, I listened with all my might. At first, the voices sounded indistinct and afar off, and the regular click of their hammers (for I am sure they were working on the stone walls of the cavern), seemed to drown their voices, but soon I became accustomed to both sounds, and could distinguish what they sang."

"What was it?" eagerly demanded the blue dragon-fly.

"I will try to remember," replied the brown beetle, and he recited slowly the following lines:

> "In their dark homes,
> Live merry gnomes.
> Through the long day,
> At home they stay,
> Their hammers ring
> Kling a ling kling.
> When others sleep,
> Abroad they peep,
> The darkest night
> Is their delight.
> Running, leaping,
> Spying, peeping,
> The dead of night
> Is gnomes' delight."

"They must be jolly fellows, and I should like to get a look at them at their work," said the blue dragon-fly, "but I wish they would take the day-time for their frolics. It would be *such* fun to watch them."

The brown beetle was silent. He wanted to tell the blue dragon-fly that he would be on the watch, and whenever he saw the gnomes he would give her all the information he gained, but he was not quick-witted, and hardly knew how to say it.

"Perhaps thou wilt be able to find out more about these strange creatures," said the blue dragon-fly. "If thou shouldst, pray let me know, for I am full of curiosity about them, they do play such fine tricks upon the giants."

Before the brown beetle could reply, the attendants of the blue dragon-fly came swarming up the hill, evidently in a state of great excitement.

"Well?" demanded their haughty mistress, for not one of them would have dared address her without permission.

"Gracious lady," began the first maid of honor, "we searched for a pool of water suitable for thy ladyship to bathe in, but the drought has affected most of those which thy ladyship is accustomed to frequent, and we were obliged to go farther away. At last, we discovered one where the water is clear and cool, where pond-lily-blossoms with their broad, green pads form suiting resting-places for our gracious lady queen."

"Why this tiresome explanation?" demanded the queen imperiously. "My province it is to command, thine to execute, not to make speeches. Lead the way."

"But, gracious lady," replied the maid of honor obsequiously, "permit me, I beg, to say a few words. A most strange thing happened, as we were contemplating the pond that was to serve as a bath for our beautiful queen. Even as we gazed, a rustling in the bushes startled us, and there appeared before our eyes a being such as we have never before beheld."

"One of the elves, thou stupid," retorted the queen sharply, "the lilies are full of them. Many and many a time, I have seen them sleeping in the lily petals and floating on the pads."

"Pardon me, gracious lady, but it was no elf; those we know well. It was a large being, and it stepped into the water and seized a lily blossom and broke it off, and another, and still another, until its large hands were full of the beautiful blossoms thy ladyship so loves to alight on."

"Nonsense, if it were not an elf, then it must have been a giant," answered the blue dragon-fly impatiently.

"It was not a giant, gracious lady," continued the maid of honor, "it was not so large. It was a being the like of which has never set its feet on these shores."

"Will wonders never cease?" exclaimed the blue dragon-fly in amazement. "What in the name of all that is marvelous could it have been?"

CHAPTER III.

WASSA'S THEFT.

The strange apparition that had so startled the attendants of the blue dragon-fly was merely a little maid. Her one garment, made from the rough skin of some animal, was torn and jagged, and presented a very untidy appearance, while her coarse black hair hung about her face in disorderly locks.

The little maid waded into the pond, and roughly pulled some of the beautiful pond lilies that floated on the surface. A rustling in the bushes caused her to turn her head, and two other little maids, younger than the first comer, and a lad, made their appearance. A strong family resemblance proclaimed them to be brother and sisters, and the skins that formed their clothes were as worn and untidy as were those of the elder sister.

"Wilt thou not throw us some of the blossoms, Wassa?" asked one of the little maids.

The one who was gathering the lilies carelessly threw a bunch toward the new-comers, and then continued her occupation.

Soon another rustling in the bushes announced the approach of some one else, and another little maid stood before them and looked about her.

The new-comer was of about the size of the one gathering lilies, but her whole appearance was different. Her dress was made of rabbit skins neatly sewed together, and she wore leggins and moccasins of leather tastefully and carefully embroidered with porcupine quills stained in bright colors. Her brown hair was neatly braided, and her dark blue eyes had an open, honest expression. She had the confiding, trusting air that is seen in children who are tenderly and carefully reared, and who have experienced only love and kindness.

The blue-eyed maid stood at some distance from the brother and sisters, and watched them with great interest, with the wistful expression one sees but in an only child; but a troubled look came over her face as Wassa ruthlessly tore the beautiful blossoms from their stems.

At last, Wassa, wading deeper into the pond, reached forward and snatched an unusually fine blossom so roughly that it broke close to the flower, at which she carelessly tossed it into the middle of the pond.

"Oh! how canst thou do that?" exclaimed the blue-eyed maid.

Wassa darted an angry glance behind her at the words of the blue-eyed maid. "Why should I not do so? How dar'st thou interfere with my pleasure?"

"It is a pity to destroy flowers thou dost not intend to care for," replied the blue-eyed maid gently.

"Why is it a pity?" asked Wassa roughly. "Flowers are not alive, they cannot feel."

"We don't know but that they may feel," replied the other; "and then, these beautiful blossoms make such splendid homes for the fairies, thou know'st."

The dark-eyed children looked at the blue-eyed maid in astonishment, then Wassa laughed loudly and derisively, and the younger children joined in.

"Fairies!" exclaimed Wassa, "how canst thou

be so stupid? I suppose thou hast seen them, hast thou not?"

"I am not quite sure," replied the blue-eyed maid gently, "but I have often looked for them, and once I was almost certain I saw a little fairy fly out of one of the blossoms, but it went so fast I couldn't say for sure."

"There are not any fairies, nor any giants, nor anything else of that kind," retorted Wassa positively, shaking her black locks.

The blue-eyed maid did not reply, much to Wassa's disappointment, for she would have liked to draw her into a quarrel.

"Dost thou mean to say thou believ'st in such nonsense?" asked Wassa.

'I believe there are fairies and giants," answered the blue-eyed maid, "although we cannot see them; and I think we ought to be very careful not to step on the flowers, nor break them off their stems unless we mean to care for them, for, for all we know, they may be the homes of fairies who love them as much as we do our own homes."

"The fairies will have to look out for their homes then," exclaimed Wassa loudly, and roughly seized all the beautiful white blossoms within her reach, and scattered them over the pond.

"Oh! how canst thou be so cruel?" cried the blue-eyed maid indignantly. "Do not destroy the pretty blossoms."

"Do thou not be so silly," answered Wassa.

"Mona! where art thou? I want thee to fetch a jug of water from the spring," called a voice in the distance.

"Yes, mother, I am coming," replied the blue-eyed maid, and she ran off quickly in the direction of the voice.

"How proud she is," exclaimed Wassa, when Mona was out of sight.

"She's proud because she has such a fine frock on," said one of the little maids.

"Dost thou not know that she's an only child?" asked Wassa contemptuously. "That's always the way with only children, they're always spoiled. But thou wilt see how long her fine airs will hold out."

"Yes, we will see!" echoed the younger children.

The blue-eyed maid, Mona, was an only child, the only one left of several others. Her parents had recently built a hut on the shore of Lily

Pond, and with much hard labor had succeeded in clearing a small patch of ground and had planted it with care, — the little maid, in her small way, helping her parents as best she could. Fish from the pond, and game from the woods, furnished them with food, and they lived a peaceful and contented life in this wilderness.

At about the same time the hunter (as we will call Mona's father) had made his home on

the shore of the pond, a rover and his family built a hut on Willow Pond, and his children they were who destroyed the lily blossoms so ruthlessly. Too indolent to prepare the rough soil for planting, as did the hunter, the rover and his family lived only on the food the ponds and woods afforded them, and, as is often the way with indolent people, felt a great dislike to their hard-working neighbors. The industry the parents of Mona displayed in felling the forest trees and uprooting stumps, to prepare a place in which to plant their seeds, was much ridiculed by the rover and his wife; and the care and love they bestowed on their one child and their solicitude to have her grow up to be a good and useful woman was considered as "spoiling" her. It never occurred to them that the *most* spoiled children are those who envy others for having what they have not themselves.

To return to the rover's children. After Mona had disappeared, Wassa turned her steps homeward, followed by her brother and sisters. As they passed the hunter's pond, Wassa went to the edge of the water, and, stooping down, drew in a net that was set in the deep water. As she landed it on the grass, two fine bass leapt and struggled to free themselves.

Wassa skilfully extricated the fishes, and, breaking a lithe twig from a tree near by, ran it through their gills. Then she threw the empty net back into the water, and proceeded on her way. The younger children looked on in astonishment.

"Thou hast made a mistake, Wassa," said her brother. "That was not our net. It belongs to the hunter."

"I know that as well as thou dost," replied Wassa, "but I intend that the hunter's family

shall have no fishes for their supper to-night. It will serve Mona right for being so proud."

"Yes, it will serve her right," assented the other children quickly, falling in with their elder sister's plan as readily as all younger children do; and home went the rover's children, without a pang of conscience at the theft they had committed.

For a while after the children had disappeared, all was still in the woods,— still as far as the noises made by human beings were concerned.

Occasionally a fish jumped in the pond, and dragon-flies skimmed over its surface,— birds flew in and out among the trees, and squirrels ran over the branches. Gradually, however, the sun sank out of sight, the notes of the birds grew shorter and more subdued, until their sleepy voices ceased altogether, and the squirrels went fast asleep in their snug nests. A refreshing coolness spread through the woods, and the evening air became laden with the perfumed breath of the forest trees. First one star and then another appeared, and the round, full moon rose from behind Blue Hill, and sailed into the sky, shedding a soft light over pond and wood and hill.

Then, dear readers, if you had but been there to see the tiny forms that sprang from beneath the large stones and from within the mounds, and that came sliding down from their homes in the hollow trees.

Each small face was brimming with mirth and good nature, and their nimble little feet flew over the ground without seeming to touch so much as a blade of grass. By hundreds they came, all flocking to the verge of the pond, where they joined hands, and executed a wild and fantastic dance, singing, at the same time, the following lines:—

> "Sleeping all day,
> At night we stray
> From our snug homes
> In trees, 'neath stones.
> On waves we ride,
> In flowers hide,
> And dance and sing
> Till the woods ring.
> But elves must work,
> Nor duty shirk;
> The good to right
> Is our delight.
> Spites to prevent
> Is our intent.
> Say, brother elves,
> Bethink yourselves,
> Knows any one
> Work to be done?"

The circle of elves danced around the pond, executing all kinds of fantastic steps, until the exuberance of their spirits was somewhat exhausted, when they bent their tiny faces over the water and gazed into its clear depths.

For a time no one spoke, until one of their band, the most dimpled and roguish-looking of them all, the most nimble of foot and graceful in the dance, Toto the Slim, thus addressed his comrades:—

"Brothers mine, the nets of the hunter lie at the bottom of this lake, as ye well know, and I crave your attention while I relate what befell this day. Hidden 'neath yon mossy stone, footsteps, human footsteps, fell on my ear, and, peeping cautiously forth, I espied Wassa, the rover's maid, with her brother and sisters. Mindful of the unkind feeling they bear the hunter's little maid, I watched them closely. Drawing the hunter's nets, they threw them on the shore, and within the meshes leapt two shining bass. These fishes these naughty children *stole*, my comrades. Now, I ask ye, brothers mine, shall we allow this deed to go unpunished? Must the gentle Mona, she who so loves the fairy folk and is so loved by them, go without her supper?"

"No, a thousand times no," cried all the

elves in chorus. "Let us at once to Wassa's hut and pay her for this naughty trick!"

"Comrades mine," said Toto the Slim, his tiny face brimful of mischief, "I, for one, do not believe in turning the other cheek, but in giving a good slap back. So, I say, let us at once repay this trick tenfold. Come on!" And Toto laughed gleefully as he gave a twirl to his mustache.

Before, however, Toto and his comrades bounded away, Pippi the Just, the oldest and wisest of the band, raised his hand with an authoritative gesture and spoke these words:—

"Toto, my friend, thou art young as yet, but thou wilt gain wisdom when thou art older. Those who take what is not their own should be made to make amends, and I counsel this, — that we look at the rover's nets, and if there should be two fishes in them, they go, by rights, to the hunter's nets. This, friend Toto, is just and right, and thou wilt find it works better than thy rule. Come, then, comrades, let us go."

Away over bush and stone went the nimble elves, nor halted until they stood on the shore of Willow Pond. The net of the rover was soon found, and, forming in line, the wee elves tugged at the lines, while the woods about echoed with their shrill voices. At last the net appeared on the surface of the water, and soon four fine bass were plunging on the grassy bank of the pond.

"Two back with the nets we'll throw," said Pippi the Just, "and two we will put in the hunter's nets."

All the elves assented to this as wise and just,— all except that mischievous elf, Toto the Slim, but no one thought of him. Then back to Lily Pond went the troops of elves carrying the two fishes, and not one of them noticed that the wag Toto was left behind.

When the last elf had disappeared among the forest trees, Toto, laughing softly to himself all the while, drew forth the rover's net once more, and opening it, out sped the two fishes, and diving to the depths of the pond, were quickly lost to view.

Next, this waggish imp gazed about with his roguish eyes until they espied two flat stones. These he rolled, with much exertion, to the edge of the pond, and, putting them into the net, cast it once more into the water.

Down to the depths of the lake went the weighted net, and a shower of spray arose, while Toto, delighted at the success of his plan, danced joyfully about, and then bounded into the woods and sought the hollow tree that served him for a home. Into this he crept, and sinking on to his bed of moss, was soon asleep.

The sun rose on a scene so peaceful and quiet that no one would have believed that hundreds of elves had made it their playground.

CHAPTER IV.

FAIRY WELL AND PLOT OF GNOMES.

The next morning the little brown beetle crawled from under a large leaf that grew on a tree near by Lily Pond, where the hunter's nets were cast, and that had served him for a roof during the night, and looked about him. He had seen the revels of the elves or fairies, and his little mind was still in a state of bewilderment, for the brown beetle's mind moved slowly, and the rapid manner in which the little elves worked quite dazed his dull, honest brain.

"It serves them right for being so envious!" exclaimed a voice, suddenly disturbing the brown beetle's revery.

The beetle was not nervous, but he had thought himself alone, and he gave a little start of surprise as he turned in the direction of the voice.

The blue dragon-fly was poised on a tall and

slender blade of grass, that hardly quivered under the light weight as she fanned her gauzy wings in order to balance herself gracefully. The swarm of gnats who attended on her hovered together in the warm air at a respectful distance from their haughty queen.

"Well!" said the dragon-fly impatiently, as the brown beetle made no reply to her remark.

The good-natured beetle looked inquiringly at the blue dragon-fly, but as he was not sure to what she referred, and therefore was ignorant as to what reply she expected him to make, wisely concluded that it was best to keep silent.

"Stupid creature!" muttered the blue dragon-fly with an angry quiver of her wings, as she said aloud: "I am waiting to see how vexed the rover's children will be when they find only stones in their net."

"Stones?" inquired the beetle mildly.

"Yes, *stones*," replied the blue dragon-fly sharply. "The stones Toto the Slim put in their nets in place of the fishes."

The brown beetle might indeed look bewildered, for all he knew about the matter was that the elves had put two *fishes* into the rover's nets. He did not know that the mischievous Toto had remained behind, and, releasing the fishes, had put two flat stones in their place.

"I was not aware of that," stammered the brown beetle; "I thought they were fishes."

"The elves were foolish enough to leave two fishes in the rover's net," answered the blue dragon-fly, "but Toto the Slim, who has more brains than all the rest put together, thought the rover's children deserved to go without any fishes at all, and after the elves had gone he remained behind, and, releasing the fishes, replaced them by two stones. Now, I am waiting to see Wassa's disappointment when she finds what the nets contain. What fun it will be, when she thinks the nets heavy with fish, to see her vexation at sight of the great flat stones!" and the dragon-fly laughed mischievously.

"It is very warm here; fan me!" ordered the dragon-fly to her maids-in-waiting, after a moment's silence.

The submissive attendants fluttered up to their queen, and fanned their wings until they succeeded in raising a slight breeze.

FAIRY WELL AND PLOT OF GNOMES. 45

"That will do," ordered the queen after a while, and the obedient maids-in-waiting retired to a respectful distance.

"Fly to the rover's lake, watch for Wassa's coming, then acquaint me," commanded the blue dragon-fly, and away swarmed the gnats.

Then the brown beetle and the blue dragon-fly heard a crackling among the dry twigs and leaves, and in a moment the branches were

thrust aside, and a light form springing through the opening stood on the shore of the pond.

It was little Mona, the hunter's child — the brown beetle, slow as was his mind, had learned to know her from the conversation of the elves, and this he communicated in a whisper to the blue dragon-fly.

The little maid stood by the pond, holding back the branches with both hands, and bending forward to gaze into the water. A very pretty picture she made, with her cap embroidered by her mother's loving fingers with porcupine quills stained in brilliant colors, her short garment of rabbit skins, and her pretty moccasins and leggins. So thought the honest brown beetle, and the blue dragon-fly thought so, too.

Soon Mona's bright eyes caught sight of the nets of which she was in search, and, quickly loosing her hold of the branches, with a light bound she reached the spot where the nets lay, and drew them ashore. The two fishes that were within plunged and leapt on the grass, and, quickly securing them, the little maid departed.

No sooner was Mona gone than the dragonfly's attendants came swarming back from the rover's pond. Something had evidently thrown them into a state of great excitement, but so strict were their rules of etiquette that nothing could have tempted them to address their queen until she had given them permission to do so.

"Well?" demanded the blue dragon-fly in a condescending tone, "what have ye to report?"

"Gracious lady," replied the first lady-in-waiting deferentially, "we followed thy commands and hovered over the lake in the vicinity of the rover's nets. Ere, long we heard the sound of approaching footsteps, and soon the rover's children appeared. 'I wish we might see Mona when she finds her nets empty,' said Wassa as she seized the cord of her own nets and began pulling them toward the shore. 'How heavy they are!' she cried as she drew them through the water; 'we shall have plenty of fishes to-day.'

"Imagine her surprise, gracious queen, when, instead of fishes, two large, flat stones lay in the nets!" She exclaimed angrily, 'This is Mona's work!' and the other children echoed, 'Yes, this is Mona's work! It is she who did the mischief.'

"Then, gracious lady, my attention was suddenly attracted by a tall, yellow lily that waved to and fro on its stem, and looking closely, I beheld the tiny face of that roguish elf, Toto the Slim. Leaping from the chalice of the lily, down the slender stalk he climbed, and, after a wild dance of exultation, away he sped."

"Return to thy story of the children," commanded the queen haughtily, and the maid of honor submissively continued her story:—

"Pardon me, my lady queen; I imagined it would be of interest to know that Toto the Slim was at the bottom of the mischief, for of that I am sure from the merry expression of his face.

"The children soon recovered from their surprise, and Wassa cried: 'We will pay the proud maid for this. We will teach her to play tricks on us.' And, gracious queen, they are now on their way hither."

No sooner had the maid of honor ceased speaking than Wassa appeared, followed by her brother and sisters. With angry haste they drew in the nets that Mona had, a few moments before, thrown into the water, and, with hands and feet, endeavored to tear them to pieces; but the nets were strongly made, and resisted their violent efforts. Then a new idea entered Wassa's mind.

"We will roll a big stone into the nets and sink them where they will never again be found," she exclaimed.

Away went the excited children in search of a stone large enough to suit their purpose, and soon espied one not far away. By dint of great pushing they at last succeeded in rolling it to the spot where the nets lay, then, twining the nets about it, they carefully pushed it to the edge of the lake.

One vigorous push, and in went the heavy stone, and the children ran quickly back to escape the shower of water that arose as the stone splashed in. In a moment more all was as still as before,—the calm surface of the lake looked as if it might keep forever the secret of the hidden nets.

After a cautious survey of the still water, and sure that no trace of their ill deed was left to betray them, the children went home, well satisfied with the success of their naughty trick.

"How spiteful they are!" exclaimed the blue

dragon-fly indignantly, "and all because they are envious of Mona and the pretty things she wears!"

> "Beware of all the passions wild,
> But the saddest of all, an envious child,"

sang a voice from above, and the tiny elf, Toto the Slim, was seen astride the limb of an oak that grew above the spots where the brown beetle and the blue dragon-fly were stationed.

"This is a pretty state of affairs!" exclaimed the blue dragon-fly. "Now, those nets of the hunter lie at the bottom of the lake and there they will stay."

> "There they will stay
> Till close of day;
> In moonbeams bright
> They'll come to light."

As Toto the Slim said these words, he slid down from the branch on which he was seated, and popped into the hollow of the tree that served as his house.

Long the blue dragon-fly and the brown beetle pondered over the words of the elf, but it meant nothing to them; for how could moonlight disclose the nets that lay at the bottom of the lake, when they could not be seen in the brighter sunlight?

While the blue dragon-fly and the brown beetle are pondering over the words of the elf Toto, we will turn to other friends.

That same night, as soon as the woods were quiet and dark, a little gnome might have been seen coming down Blue Hill. Bounding over stones and bushes, swinging on grapevines, leaping across streams and chasms, on went the little gnome until he reached the hollow tree in which dwelt the elf Toto the Slim. Standing at the foot of the tree, the gnome called out: —

> "Wake up, wake up, friend elf, I pray,
> And hear the words I have to say."

No sooner were these words spoken than the rosy, roguish face of Toto appeared at the opening that led to his snug home, and in a trice he slid down the tree and alighted at the gnome's feet, saying: —

"At thy service, little gnome,
So prithee say wherefore thou'st come."

The gnome made an answer thus:—

"Toto the Slim, I have a plan, to which I hope thou wilt agree. There are two things that weigh on my mind greatly. One is, to see the envy that is in Wassa's heart toward the hunter's little maid, whom we all love, and who has not deserved such unkind treatment at Wassa's hands. The other is, the best way to avenge the insults our giant enemies constantly put upon us. Now, I have bethought me of a plan to kill two birds with one stone and settle both of these matters at the same time. How would it do to have the giants, when the rover's family are fast asleep, lift up the hut and bear it with its inmates far away, where they will never trouble Mona more? Now, this will relieve the hunter's little maid of all annoyances, and will get the giants into trouble, for thou know'st they may do nothing unless ordered by the little gray man. What think'st thou of my plan, friend elf?"

"Thy plan is excellent, friend gnome," replied Toto the Slim, always ready to fall in with any project that promised mischief.

'One difficulty alone occurs to me. The giants on whom thou hast practised so many tricks will at once suspect thee of a snare to entrap them. Thou wilt have to find some messenger whom they will believe."

"Of that I have thought," replied the gnome, "and I have provided for it. The blue dragon-fly is on friendly terms with the giants, and would be a fitting messenger. Say'st thou not so?"

" None better," said Toto the Slim.

" Then the sooner I see her the better," replied the gnome, " so good night, friend elf."

Away sped the gnome on his mischievous errand, and the elf crept back to his bed, where he soon slept soundly once more.

The next day the blue dragon-fly called pettishly to her attendants, " Knows any one the whereabouts of the giants to-day?"

" May it please thy ladyship," began the first lady-in-waiting, "we heard that the giants have found the heat so oppressive that they departed this morning for the sea-shore, to wade about in the channel, hoping to refresh themselves after the restless night they had passed."

"Very well," replied the blue dragon-fly, waving them back, "then I will await their return. Follow me."

Away flew the dragon-fly, followed at a respectful distance by her attendants.

So light was the blue dragon-fly, and so strong her gauzy wings, that before long she reached Blue Hill that she knew to be the headquarters of the giants. As she soared up the hill, she all at once heard the regular click of hammers, and the sound of voices keeping time with the blows. As she approached, she saw, on the side of the hill that looks toward the setting sun and which, then as now, reflected his last rays, hundreds of little gnomes at work with their tiny hammers.

Sturdy of limb, with peaked caps, peaked beards, and grave faces, the little band worked industriously away, and the blue dragon-fly lighted on a tree near by, and listened to the song they sang: —

> "Spirit of yon leafy dell,
> Grant, we beg, a fairy well.
> May its waters, fresh as dew,
> Flow only for the good and true.
> Should the bad and false pass by,

Be for them this fountain dry.
Should an envious face peer in,
Reflect, we pray, with all its sin.
The horror of an envious mind,
Of all sad sights, the worst we find,
And what grieves most the fairies mild,
The manners of an envious child."

As the song ceased, the gnomes paused in

their work, and all gazed toward the meadows that lay below, and through which a stream ran like a silver thread. A white mist, through which a delicate form was faintly seen, rose from the water, and, seeming to bend toward the Blue Hill, gradually floated away and faded in the distance.

At the instant the last wreath of mist disappeared, a gurgling of water was heard, and from the rock where the gnomes had been at work there gushed a stream of water clear as crystal, and filled the basin that had been made.

Whereupon the little gnomes made obeisance toward the place where the spirit of the dell had appeared, while they uttered these words: —

> "Thanks, fair spirit of yon dell,
> For granting us a fairy spell.
> May this sparkling little rill
> Refresh those travelling up Blue Hill;
> But should the envious come this way,
> Help them to cure their fault, we pray."

As they ended, the gnomes shouldered their little hammers and ascended the hill in single file, the blue dragon-fly gazing with amazement after their retreating figures.

"Can I have been dreaming?" asked the

blue dragon-fly of herself. No, she could not have been, for there was the newly hewn well full of clear water."

"Now, if envious Wassa could look in, what a picture she would see!" thought the blue dragon-fly.

A distant rumbling was now heard.

"There are no clouds in the sky, so it can't be thunder," said the blue dragon-fly to herself. "It must be the giants laughing. It is fortunate for me that they are in a good humor."

Nearer and nearer came the rumbling, and soon the blue dragon-fly could distinguish the loud "ha — ha — ha!" of the big fellows, and before long their great forms came into view. The dragon-fly watched them as, one by one, they jumped across the pond that lay in their path, and a few strides brought them to the hill.

As the giants strode up the hill, the blue dragon-fly flew toward them, and lighted on the hand of the foremost.

"Ho, ho! my little lady, is that you?" roared King Cloudcatcher, holding the tiny creature before him, and as he spoke his breath raised such a breeze that she was nearly blown off his huge hand.

CHAPTER V.

WASSA MAKES A PLAN.

"What can we do for thee?" asked the giant king good-naturedly.

The dragon-fly lost no time in acquainting the giant with the task assigned to him, and ended her tale by begging him to avenge the tricks played upon the hunter's family.

"What wouldst thou have us do?" asked King Cloudcatcher, who was as dull-witted as his subjects.

"Take up the rover's hut and carry it as far away as those mountains yonder," replied the blue dragon-fly promptly, nodding her little head in the direction of the dim line of mountains outlined against the distant horizon.

"Our master might not be pleased, little lady," answered the giant, "if we did that without his bidding."

"I should think you were big enough to be your own masters," said the blue dragon-fly sarcastically.

"Our bodies are big and so are our heads," replied the giant, "but the master says they contain very little brains. It might bring trouble upon us, lady-bird, to do as thou wishest."

"I will take the responsibility," said the blue dragon-fly loftily.

The giant king laughed so loudly at this boastful speech of the blue dragon-fly that the little creature was blown suddenly off his great finger. She soon recovered her balance, however, and alighted at a safe distance upon a bush that grew near by. The other giants joined in their king's mirth, and the hill reverberated with their loud laughter.

"Yes," repeated the blue dragon-fly, when silence was restored, "I will take the responsibility. What is there so amusing in that? What harm can come from doing my bidding? Two of ye can take up the hut with the rover's family inside, and set it down again before they know what has happened."

"The little lady is right, by my faith," said one of the giants; "there can be no harm in it."

It was decided that after the moon had risen

that evening two of the strongest and most reliable giants should lift the rover's hut and bear it so far away that the hunter's family should suffer no more persecutions at their hands.

As soon as this plan was agreed upon, the blue dragon-fly flew home, followed by her attendants, who had all this time remained obediently near.

The day deepened into afternoon, and the sun set behind the western woods; twilight came on with its soft shadows, and at last the moon rose over the eastern brow of Blue Hill and sailed into the sky, lighting up the meadows and casting a silver sheen over the winding river. Sometimes the shining stream seemed lost amid the tangle of trees and shrubs, but there it was again, glistening brighter than ever in the clear moonlight.

No noise was heard save the chirping of crickets and tree-toads, and the occasional cry of a night hawk. Then down Blue Hill came the giants, and strode toward the pond on whose shores the rover's hut stood.

Half hidden by trees was the hut, built of trees and boughs roughly put together. It

WASSA MAKES A PLAN. 61

was a very crude affair, and all the light that entered came through the open door.

The two giants who were to carry away the hut cautiously approached, and stooping down, looked in through the open door. The inside of the hut was as untidy as was the outside, and the giants saw the rover's family fast asleep on beds of fir boughs.

Satisfied that everything was in readiness for their plan, the giants rose to their feet and

prepared to begin their work, while their companions stationed themselves at a distance to watch the proceeding.

The two giants bent over to raise the hut from the ground, but no sooner had they placed their hands under the rude structure than a voice was heard to say: —

"Hold, ye knaves! What is it ye are about to do?"

The two giants quickly straightened themselves to their full height and looked about them. Standing on a rock near by was the little gray man, who looked sternly at them.

"The blue dragon-fly told us to. We did it but to please her," the giants hastened to say.

"Is the blue dragon-fly your mistress? Have ye sworn obedience to her?" demanded the little man in gray.

"Pardon, master," they humbly answered, "but the rover's family persecute the honest hunter, and we thought to remove them out of their reach. We meant no harm."

"Your duty is to obey, mine to command," sternly replied the little gray man. "Do thou, Deepdrinker, follow me."

The giant thus designated meekly followed his master to the shores of Lily Pond, in whose depths Wassa had sunken the hunter's nets, and the little gray man commanded: —

"Drain the pond at one draught."

The huge giant threw himself prostrate on

the ground, and, taking a deep breath, put his lips into the water and drank deeply. Gradually the water receded from the margin of the pond, and the giant drank on, until the muddy basin was disclosed, and in it the large stone around which Wassa had twisted the hunter's nets.

"Thou hast done well, Deepdrinker; it was a goodly draught," said the little gray man. "Rockroller, come hither."

Another giant stepped out from among his companions, and approached the edge of the pond as Deepdrinker arose to his feet.

"Reach out thy hand, Rockroller, free the nets, and toss yon pebble over the hill," again commanded the little gray man.

The giant did as he was bidden, extricated carefully the nets that had been twisted about the large stone, and then, lifting the stone between his thumb and finger, as if it had indeed been a pebble, tossed it lightly over Blue Hill.

"Swiftstepper, do thou take the nets and put them in their proper places," commanded the little gray man, "and then back to bed, ye sleepy heads."

The little gray man vanished as suddenly

as he had appeared, and Swiftstepper, standing with one foot on each shore of the pond, carefully replaced the hunter's nets, as the little gray man had bidden, and then he rejoined his companions.

It was fortunate for the safety of the gnomes that the giants did not discover the little faces with their peaked beards and caps peeping out from behind bushes and rocks, watching with mischievous enjoyment the success of their plot; and still more fortunate was it that they did not hear the shrill, jeering laughs that arose at the sharp reproof of the little man in gray.

Great was Wassa's surprise, the next morning, at finding the hunter's nets cast in the usual place.

"Perhaps the fairies did it," suggested one of her little sisters.

"Nonsense! there are no fairies, I tell thee," replied Wassa angrily. "How dost thou suppose fairies could get that great rock out of the water?"

"Then maybe the giants did it," said the brother.

"There are no giants either; thou know'st that as well as I," replied Wassa.

"I saw something one day that looked just like a fairy," said the youngest sister timidly. "It looked like a tiny face peeping out of a pond lily."

"'Twas a dragon-fly or a butterfly, thou little goose," replied Wassa. "Thou art as foolish as Mona to imagine thou see'st fairies."

"Who dost thou think took the nets and stone out of the pond?" asked the brother.

"The witches, I suppose," replied Wassa with a laugh.

"There is Mona now," said one of the little maids, pointing in the direction of the hunter's hut.

Through the tall forest trees the children saw Mona busily at work in her little garden. She had transplanted with much pains many of the prettiest wild flowers, and columbine and violets and innocence were blooming as freshly and cheerfully as if they had sprung up of their own accord.

"See how proud the little maid is," whispered the brother; "dost thou not see how careful she is not to spoil her fine clothes?"

"If it were not for her fine clothes, she wouldn't look any better than any one else."

answered Wassa angrily. "See that silly cap perched on the top of her head! I wish we could get it away from her!"

"I'll snatch it off the next time I see her," said the lad.

"No, no, thou must not do that," replied Wassa. "Let me think."

Wassa was silent for a few minutes, then she resumed, with a meaning nod toward Mona:—

"I know how to manage it. Thou shalt see how easily I will arrange matters," and away ran Wassa toward Mona at work in her little garden.

The two little maids and their brother left behind had such unbounded confidence in Wassa that they were not surprised to see Mona, after a few words, follow Wassa with a smiling countenance.

The hunter's little maid was so much by herself that she was overjoyed at the prospect of playmates, and Wassa was usually so unfriendly that Mona was very glad to find her in so gracious a mood.

The younger children could not understand why Wassa should so suddenly be on such cordial terms with the hunter's maid, but they always fell in with her moods, and soon all the children were playing happily together.

Mona, who had always been obliged to play by herself, was particularly happy at finding the rover's children so affable, and was ready to believe that their natures had undergone a change, and that henceforth all was to be peace and sunshine. Her gay laughter rang merrily through the woods, and her play was the wildest of all.

Farther and farther from home strayed the children, led on by Wassa, until Mona, breathless from a wild chase, was startled to find herself where she had never before been.

"I must go home directly," cried Mona anxiously; "my mother will think we are lost."

"There is no hurry," replied Wassa confidently; "we are at the foot of Blue Hill, and we may as well ascend it, for we shall have time to reach home before sundown. I know the way very well, and it will take but a little while."

"I don't dare," replied Mona; "my mother is always anxious if I am away long. Some other time, dear Wassa, I shall be glad to go with thee."

"Thou canst not go until I do," replied Wassa, "for thou dost not know the way. Thou wilt get lost, and the bears come out at night, and they will eat thee up. So thou see'st, thou mayst as well have the pleasure of going up the hill."

At these words Wassa began to ascend the footpath made by the feet of the giants, her brother and sisters closely following her. The hunter's little maid hesitated for a moment, and then reluctantly joined the party.

Mona's nature was a happy one, and when she considered that the only course left her was to keep with the rover's children, she resolved to make the best of the matter; so whenever the thought of home and her mother came into her mind, she put it resolutely aside.

Up the hill roamed the children, stopping occasionally to pick the blueberries that grew in thick clusters on each side of the path, or to peer into the numerous caves they passed, half expecting to see some strange animal spring out at them. When about half way up the hill they came upon the fairy-well the gnomes had so lately made.

"Oh! what beautiful clear water!" exclaimed the hunter's little maid. "I can see my face there, it is so clear;" and all the children crowded around to catch a glimpse of themselves.

"Let me look!" cried Wassa, coming from behind and looking over the heads of the other children.

What a picture was seen in the clear surface of the fairy-well, dear readers! Above the head of Mona with her pretty cap and the happy faces of the younger children, appeared the face of Wassa, but how transfigured by the magic well! Reflected in the clear water, so changed was the countenance with its distorted features and complexion of green, that the other children started back in terror, and gazed at their sister to see what had brought about so sudden a change.

No, Wassa's face had not changed. What they saw was wrought by the spell of the spirit of the dell.

"How dreadful thy picture in the water is,' said one of the little maids; "it looks as if thou wast making up a face, and thy complexion is all green."

"I *did* make up a face," replied Wassa, who had a secret misgiving that the spring was reflecting the envious thoughts that filled her breast. "Come, let us go farther on, or we cannot be home before dark."

On went the children once more, when Wassa suddenly walked to the edge of the path and looked down. "Just see how steep the side of the hill is," she exclaimed, beckoning to the children.

Cautiously the others approached and gazed down the steep hillside. The path was indeed steep, and many large rocks lay in the way. As Mona leant forward to peep over, Wassa, as if by accident, pushed roughly against her. Mona's light cap fell off, and in spite of her quick efforts to recover it, the cap was borne swiftly over the precipice.

"My cap! My cap!" cried Mona anxiously; "I must go after it."

"Thou must not think of such a thing," said Wassa decidedly. "There it lies at the foot of the precipice, and thou couldst never climb up again, even if thou shouldst manage to go safely down."

"But I *must*," replied Mona. "I cannot lose the pretty cap my mother took such pains to make for me."

"It will very soon be dark, and I am going home. Come, children," said Wassa.

So saying, Wassa started to return, followed by her brother and sisters. Looking back, they saw Mona beginning cautiously to descend the steep path.

"What art thou doing, Mona?" called Wassa sharply.

"I am going to find my cap," replied the little maid resolutely.

"Thou wilt never find thy way home, and when it is dark the bears will come out and eat thee," said Wassa. "My father says he has often seen them prowling about at night."

Wassa thought this threat would induce Mona to give up her project, but she was mistaken. Mona valued the cap highly, both for the sake of her mother, who had taken great pleasure in making it for her little daughter, and also because it was so pretty, and, moreover, she was not a timid child.

Wassa watched the light figure of the little maid as she began the descent. Carefully she caught the boughs that came in her way, and held them firmly to steady herself down the steep declivity. When they had watched her half way down, the children turned their steps homeward, leaving Mona to her fate.

"I did all I could to persuade her to come with us, did I not?" asked Wassa, as the children walked rapidly down the hill.

"Yes, certainly thou didst," they answered, "but she would not listen to thee."

In fact, Wassa did not intend that her trick in knocking off Mona's cap should have so disastrous an ending, and she felt somewhat frightened at the result. Influenced by her jealousy, she was determined to cause Mona's pretty cap to disappear forever, but she had not thought that the gentle little maid would dare venture down the steep ravine to recover it.

Meanwhile the sun was sinking lower and lower, and the little maid was continuing her way down the rough hillside.

CHAPTER VI.

THE ELVES AND GNOMES TO THE RESCUE

With a fast-beating heart little Mona began to descend the precipice. She hoped to recover the cap and overtake her companions before they were out of hearing, but she did not realize the extent of the task she had undertaken.

Looking down from the edge of the precipice, the distance to the bottom did not seem very great, but the path was rough and steep, and Mona made very slow progress. Seizing for her support the longest boughs within reach, the little maid carefully selected a secure footing before releasing the bough. Often the loose earth gave way as she set her foot upon it, and fell crashing down the hillside, and then it seemed as if the task were almost hopeless, and the cap looked as far off as when she first started.

The cap hung on the top of a fir tree that, from where the little maid stood, looked no higher than a bush of medium size, but in reality it was a tall tree that had been growing for several generations.

Mona had plenty of courage, and not once did she think of giving up her project; but as the sun sank lower and lower, and she realized how very little headway she had made, a dreadful misgiving took possession of her. " What if she should not reach the bottom of the hill before dark?" Next came the thought, " What if the bears did really go prowling about at night?"

" I will not think of such things," said the brave little maid to herself. " I will think of the kind fairies. Perhaps there are some about here, and they are watching me now."

This last pleasant thought reassured the little wanderer, and she cheered herself by imagining the flowers and trees about her peopled by the small beings she had learned to love. If she could but have seen the tiny faces that peeped after her from their leafy hiding-places, she would have felt secure in the thought that she was not alone.

Bushes heavy with their weight of blueberries were on either side, and wild flowers grew under her footsteps, but Mona did not stop to pick any, fearing the sun might go out of sight before she reached the top of the hill again. Soon, to her great joy, the foot of the hill, where the cherished cap hung on the fir tree, seemed nearer and nearer, and, looking back on the path down which she had gone so slowly and with so much difficulty, she was surprised to see how steep and how far off the summit of the precipice was. This gave the little maid new hope, and she proceeded more resolutely than ever.

As Mona was feeling about with one foot for a foothold on which to trust her weight, a sudden noise from behind arrested her attention, and she started violently, fearing that one of the bears of which Wassa had spoken had indeed come in search of her; and, losing her

THE ELVES AND GNOMES TO THE RESCUE. 77

hold by which she had supported herself, the earth on which she stood gave way, and, with a loud report that vibrated through the silent woods, it rolled swiftly down the steep hillside, carrying with it the terrified little maid.

In her fall, the thought of home and parents passed rapidly through Mona's mind, but almost before she fully realized the danger of her situation, the slide that bore her was arrested by a clump of bushes, and she was thrown into their leafy arms. The sudden shock, together with the fatigue and anxiety she had undergone, was too much for the poor little maid, and all consciousness forsook her.

No sooner did Mona's eyes close than at once every flower and shrub and tree seemed alive with the tiny faces of elves. Small faces popped out of the flowers, and slender forms came sliding down from the tall flower stalks and flowering bushes. Some seized the delicate stems of the blue hare-bell and wild lily of the valley, and rang the little bells violently. Others blew long blasts on the wild honeysuckle and columbine, while above the din shrill voices clamored excitedly.

From every direction came tiny elves crowding and pushing and stumbling over one another in their eagerness to learn the cause of this sudden summons.

Suddenly the murmur of voices ceased as they discovered the form of the hunter's little maid lying on the ground, with closed eyes and all the color gone out of her face. For a few minutes all were silent, then Lippo, the elfin king, pointing solemnly to the little form on the ground, said: —

> "Good subjects mine, here have we come
> On nimble feet, from leafy home,
> A gentle deed of love to do
> For this fair maid, so kind and true.
> Lured forth was she from her fond home
> By false words of the jealous one.
> Whate'er we do must be done soon,
> The night is short, and yon's the moon."

As the king ceased, the full, round moon slowly appeared above the tall forest trees, and moved majestically higher into the sky.

Then said Pippi the Just, the wise counsellor: —

"We tiny elves cannot by ourselves bear this gentle maid up the steep side of the mountain. The gnomes, so sturdy of limb and sure of foot, will know how to help us. Who of ye will hie to King Rondo and acquaint him with the mishap?"

Almost before the last words were spoken, Beppo, the swift of foot, was half way up the steep mountain side, on his errand to King Rondo.

Bounding over stones and bushes, climbing

nimbly over rocks, the swift-footed Beppo went on his way, until he stood before the wall of rock that formed the entrance to King Rondo's domains. Upon it, picking up a small stone for the purpose, he loudly knocked.

No answer came, and, putting his ear to the rock, the elf could hear the click of hammers ringing within, and the voices of the gnomes keeping time to the blows. Again and again Beppo repeated his knock, each time more loudly, until at last the heavy door swung back, and a gnome stood before him.

"What dost thou wish, friend Beppo?" demanded the gnome.

"It is with the king I wish to speak," replied Beppo, "on most important business, and I beg him to grant me an interview without delay."

"Enter," replied the gnome, "and I will acquaint his majesty with thy message."

The elf entered the cavern, and as the rocky door rolled back into place Beppo became sensible of a most savory odor proceeding from the depths of the cavern. This the elf knew was a favorable sign, for it was well known that King Rondo was fond of

THE ELVES AND GNOMES TO THE RESCUE. 81

good cheer, and was always in a gracious mood when eating his favorite viands.

The gnome disappeared within the king's apartments, and soon reappeared, saying: —

"His majesty bids thee enter the banquet hall, as thy message is an urgent one. He is

engaged in eating his favorite repast of "grubs on toast," and dislikes to leave them, as when cold they are tasteless and tough."

"As his majesty wills," answered the elf, following the gnome.

The door of the banquet hall was thrown open as they approached, and the sudden brilliancy before him almost blinded the little elf's eyes. The walls, hewn from solid rock, glistened with crystals and mica and garnets that reflected the light from myriads of torches.

At a table, in the midst of this splendor, sat King Rondo, eating from a smoking dish of "grubs on toast," and drinking deep draughts of "Mountain Dew," collected by his faithful subjects.

A goodly king was "Rondo the Round." Where else could be found such a red-cheeked, jolly sprite, with his fat, round body and plump, short limbs? Just to gaze on him was enough to make one happy, and to see him with his favorite dish before him, — well, words can hardly express what a pleasant sight it was.

Looking up, the king caught sight of his guest, who stood modestly in the doorway, waiting for permission to enter.

The king spoke thus: —

> "Come hither, friend, I pray thee tell
> If brother Lippo fares him well,
> And if there's aught that we can do
> To prove to him our friendship true."

Then Beppo stepped into the banquet hall, and bowing low before the king, made answer: —

"King Lippo is well, your majesty, and sends greeting. He bade me bring word of a misfortune that has befallen the hunter's little maid."

Then Beppo, in as few words as possible, related the tale of Mona's mishap through the treachery of the rover's maid, and begged the gnome king to send help to the unfortunate child.

"Return to thy king," said Rondo as the elf ended his tale, "and say to him that King Rondo will make the case his own. What ho there, knaves!" he cried to his attendant gnomes, "have the secret underground passages well lighted up, that the little maid need have no fear."

Beppo waited for no second bidding, but, saluting the king, hastened homeward. Before he left the cavern, he saw that it was one blaze of light. Passages led in every direction from the lofty cavern, and these were ablaze with the light of torches and glittering ore.

CHAPTER VII.

FAIRYLAND.

Beppo left the gnomes' cavern and hastened to carry back to King Lippo the news that the gnomes would come to the rescue of the hunter's little maid. As soon as he had left the cavern, hundreds of gnomes issued forth and came trooping down the hill. Leaping and running, they hurried along until they reached the spot where Mona lay.

Silently the gnomes crowded around the little maid, gazing fondly on her whom they had long loved. After a while King Rondo broke the silence thus: —

> "Bestir yourselves, my subjects true,
> And do the work ye've come to do."

The gnomes hastened to obey their king, and disappeared into the woods, singing:—

> "Gather, gnomes, with toil and care,
> Boughs of hemlock and balsams rare.
> Fragrant branches and flowers wild
> Deck the couch of the hunter's child.
> Gently lift her, and softly bear
> Through fairy paths the maiden fair."

Almost as soon as the last words of the

refrain had died on the air, the gnomes reappeared. Some dragged after them large boughs, and sturdy forms bent beneath the fragrant green burdens they bore on their shoulders. Throwing to the ground the boughs they had collected, the gnomes skilfully fashioned a litter, over which the elves scattered bright and fragrant wild flowers.

When the task was completed, the gnomes, at the bidding of King Rondo, gently lifted the hunter's little maid on to the soft litter, and some of the strongest of the band raised it from the ground and carefully bore it up the hill, followed by the rest of the troupe.

Slowly and cautiously went the little gnomes up the rough hillside, until they reached the rocky wall that formed the entrance to their cave. King Rondo gave the signal, the heavy door rolled back, and the procession entered the cavern.

> "Welcome, welcome, maiden dear,
> Never mortal entered here.
> Beloved by all our fairy band,
> We welcome thee to Fairyland.
> But ope thy eyes and gaze around,
> And see how fair 'tis underground."

At these words the maiden's eyes unclosed, and she gazed about her. The brilliant light of the torches, reflected a thousand-fold by the crystals and shining mica and precious stones that adorned the cavern, at first dazzled Mona's eyes, and she started from her couch. Her next glance fell on the friendly faces of the gnomes, and, so accustomed was she to think lovingly of the fairy-folk, that Fairyland had always seemed near to her, and she was not at all startled to find herself there. The welcoming words of the gnomes would have reassured her if she had been at all apprehensive, and she sank back upon her soft couch, soothed by loving words and fragrant odors, and allowed herself to be gently borne onward.

Through grottos was the little maid borne, where clear streams of water flowed over shining white sand, and in which brilliant gold and silver fishes sported. Then the wondering child passed through beautiful gardens, from whose rocky sides grew luxuriant ferns, while above her head hung spreading vines and blossoming boughs, where bright-plumaged birds flitted filling the air with sweet melody.

Sometimes through long and narrow passages was the little maid carried, but from every nook and corner kindly faces peeped out, and unseen hands showered on her as she passed handfuls of shining stones and gorgeously tinted flowers.

At length, the gnomes bearing the couch paused before a massive wall, and as it gradually rolled back Mona perceived the starlit sky above her, and breathed the breath of the woods she knew and loved so well, while voices sang: —

> "Farewell, farewell, maiden dear,
> Never, never more we fear
> Wilt thou enter Fairyland.
> But this know, — all of cur band
> Watch o'er thee by night and day,
> And safely guide thy steps alway."

As the words of the song died away, Mona found herself alone before her father's hut. Not a gnome of all the hundreds who had surrounded her was to be seen, and the thought came to her that she had been dreaming; but her eyes fell on the litter upon which she had been borne through Fairyland, and in her lap lay the beautiful flowers and brilliant stones which had been showered upon her. Eager to relate to her mother her strange adventures,

Mona hastened home, to be greeted with the question: —

"My dear, where hast thou been so long?

Thy father has been hunting the woods far and wide. What has happened to thee?"

"I have been to Fairyland, mother dear, and oh! it was so beautiful!"

The mother gazed at her little daughter in amazement, fearing her mind must have become unsettled.

"*I* thought it was a dream at first," replied Mona, answering her mother's anxious look, "but it was not. See, mother dear, what the kind fairies gave me," and she poured her treasures into her mother's lap.

More astonished still was the good hunter's wife as she saw the sparkling stones that glittered in the moonlight, and perceived the delicious fragrance of the beautiful flowers that surely could have grown nowhere but in Fairyland.

"Thou must tell me all thou hast seen," said the amazed mother.

"I was playing in my little garden," began Mona, "and Wassa came to me and asked me, oh! so pleasantly, to play with her and her brother and sisters. She has always been so rude to me that it made me very happy to see her so good-natured, and I went with her. We played and we played, and it was so nice to have somebody to play with, mother dear, that I didn't think how far away from home I was until I found myself at the foot of the hill.

"So far from home?" asked the mother reproachfully.

"I did not know, I was so busy playing, that we had gone so far, but since we were there, it did seem a pity not to go up the hill. Then what dost thou think Wassa did to me?" asked Mona, glad, like many another child, to have some one to share the blame with. "She knocked my pretty cap off, and it fell down to the bottom of a great steep hill, and I went down to get it, but I couldn't find it, and Wassa ran off and left me and then I tumbled down the hill."

"Why, thou hast thy cap on thy head," said the mother.

"Then the good little fairies must have found it for me," replied Mona. "Dost thou not think it very wrong for Wassa to knock it off? I will pay her for it though. She has always been very unkind to me."

"Dost thou think that the way to make her feel kindly to thee? I think thou know'st a much better way. But thou hast not told me about thy visit to Fairyland."

Then Mona related her descent down the steep hillside to recover her cap, and her fall, and described her awakening in the beautiful cavern and hearing the song of welcome sung by the good-hearted gnomes. She told her astonished mother of the grottos where the gold and silver fishes sported, and of the lovely flowers that bloomed all about her, and of the unseen hands that showered the sparkling stones and bright flowers over her. She ended her tale with the verse sung by the fairies, in which they promised to watch over her and protect her always.

"And dost thou think, my little maid, that the good fairies will love thee so well if thou hast revengeful thoughts toward Wassa?" asked the mother. "Thou wilt be happier if thou cherishest no ill will toward her. Give her some of thy pretty shining stones and of these beautiful bright flowers, the like of which never grew in our woods."

It was a hard struggle for the little maid to decide to do as her mother wished, for the recollection of many an unkind word rose in her memory; but her mother had always taught Mona to conquer all unkind thoughts before she went to sleep at night, and as she lay awake on her bed of boughs she tried to bring her mind to do as her mother advised.

The soft air, laden with the sweet breath of the forest trees, came in through the open cabin door, and seemed to whisper soothing words; the full moon shone mildly down on the little bed, as if she felt a mother's care; the crickets chirped cheerfully, as if to sing the little maid to sleep. All these helped to influence the child who so loved mother Nature. The struggle that was going on in Mona's mind ceased, the scales turned in the right direction, and she made a vow to do as her mother wished.

As soon as her decision was made, Mona breathed a deep sigh of relief, the restlessness ceased, and sleep closed the tired eyelids.

The next morning Mona slept later than usual, and the sun was high in the heavens when she awoke. Starting up quickly, she took a refreshing bath in the brook that ran by the hunter's cabin, and then ate the simple breakfast her mother had prepared for her. Afterwards, selecting some of the finest of her pretty stones and the brightest of her flowers, she set off in the direction of the rover's hut.

Before the little maid had gone far, she

descried the rover's children on the shore of Willow Pond, amusing themselves by throwing pebbles into the water. As soon as they saw Mona, they looked at each other in amazement, for on her head was the pretty cap that they thought would lie forever at the foot of the precipice. So embarrassed was Wassa that she did not know what to say, and stammered confusedly: —

"So thou didst find thy cap after all? How didst thou find thy way back?"

"The kind fairies brought me back," answered Mona smilingly.

"Dost thou think thou canst make me believe that?" asked Wassa.

"Look here!" cried Mona, giving Wassa the pretty stones and flowers. "Wilt thou not believe it now? The good, kind fairies gave me these."

Wassa gazed in amazement at the gifts Mona thrust into her hands, for she knew well the woods about did not produce such flowers, but she did not like to acknowledge that she had been mistaken, and that, after all, there were such beings as fairies. When, however, she heard the strange adventures of the hunter's little maid, and listened to her description of the beautiful things she had seen, Wassa's mind began to waver. A longing seized her to see for herself the wonders of Fairyland, and bring away some of the treasures it contained. In vain did she question Mona about the path that led to the entrance of Fairyland; but the hunter's little maid could only reply that she knew nothing of the path,— that her first glimpse of Fairyland was the brilliantly lighted cave.

"I know thou canst tell me if thou wilt," said Wassa, "but I will hunt until I find it. Be sure I will discover the path."

Day after day Wassa spent in roaming over the hill in the neighborhood of the spot where Mona's cap had fallen, and day after day she returned home without having gained any information.

One day Wassa's attention was attracted by a beautiful blue dragon-fly that hovered over her head as if it would alight. Sometimes it came so near that the little maid's quick hand almost closed over the fragile creature, but it always escaped just as it seemed within her grasp.

This blue dragon-fly was no other than the haughty queen whom the little brown beetle so much admired.

The dragon-fly was so persistent in keeping out of Wassa's reach, that the little maid determined to have it at any cost, and followed it farther and farther up the hill.

At last, quite out of breath, and heated, Wassa sank upon a mossy bank to rest. Tired from her fruitless chase of the blue dragon-fly, the little maid's eyes closed, and she was on the point of falling asleep, when a tiny voice, that she at first supposed to proceed from a locust or some other singing insect, attracted her attention, and as she listened she heard these words : —

> "What thou seek'st, we fairies know.
> Farther up the hill then go,
> Till near the top a maple tree,
> Tall and straight as it can be,
> Stands before a lofty rock,
> Where thou loud and long must knock."

Wassa looked quickly in the direction of the voice, but nothing was to be seen but a large "Jack-in-the-pulpit," in which a large brown beetle was quietly seated. The little maid did not see what the brown beetle saw, — the tiny elfin face hidden deep in the flower, and who had spoken the words that had startled her.

Although Wassa could not discover the being who had spoken the words she wanted to hear, she resolved to follow the directions, and at once continued her way up the hill, the blue dragon-fly flitting before, sometimes disappearing, and again returning to circle about her head.

In this manner the summit of the hill was reached, and Wassa, tired from her rapid journey, and excited at the bold step she was to take, sat down to rest and look about her. Never before had she been to the very top of the hill, and she gazed in bewilderment at the great world before her.

Miles of woodland stretched away to the beautiful blue ocean, with innumerable ponds and streams between, while far away in the distance rose the dim peaks of high mountains. From this scene Wassa's gaze came back to objects near at hand, — sturdy fir trees and lofty pines. Then her eyes fell on a tall, straight maple tree that stood in front of her.

Behind it rose a massive wall of rock, and, as Wassa recognized it, the same voice she had heard before again repeated the lines: —

> "What thou seek'st, we fairies know.
> Farther up the hill then go,
> Till near the top a maple tree,
> Tall and straight as it can be,
> Stands before a lofty rock,
> Where thou loud and long must knock."

As the voice ceased, Wassa rose, and gathering all her courage, approached the rock and knocked timidly upon it.

CHAPTER VIII.

WASSA GOES TO FAIRYLAND.

As the huge door of rock rolled back, Wassa was prepared to see the brilliantly lighted cave described by Mona; but, to her surprise, instead of finding her eyes dazzled by a flood of light, she looked upon a dimly-lighted cavern, in which her eyes, accustomed to the bright sunlight, could hardly see. A voice close beside her spoke these words: —

> "If land of fairies thou wouldst seek,
> With whom is it thou wouldst speak?"

"Is this dark place Fairyland?" asked Wassa. "I thought it was bright and full of sparkling stones and flowers."

> "All things in Fairyland, thou'lt find,
> Reflect the colors of the mind,"

replied the voice that had spoken before, and now, for the first time, Wassa beheld a little man with a comical peaked cap and a long beard standing before her.

> "Pray step within and look around.
> What each deserves, that will be found,"

said the gnome, with a mischievous twinkle of the eyes.

Wassa stepped over the threshold, and the heavy door of rock rolled back into place.

"This must be but the entrance to the beautiful light cave Mona spoke of," thought Wassa as she stumbled over a stone that in the dim light she had not seen.

"I want some of the shining stones and pretty flowers thou gav'st to Mona," said Wassa, and take me to the same beautiful places to which thou hast taken her."

The gnome replied: —

> "First ask permission of our king;
> Without that thou canst do no thing."

"Then take me quickly to him," said Wassa, "for I don't want to stay any longer in this poky old place."

> "Look where thou step and follow me,
> And soon King Rondo thou shalt see,"

said the gnome.

Wassa did as she was bidden, but in the darkness she made many a false step, and several times she fell down; but the gnome did not look behind him, and Wassa was on her feet again in a twinkling. At last, after groping about in the darkness for some time, the gnome stopped before another rocky door, and at a signal from him the door opened, and a blaze of light greeted Wassa. So brilliant was it that the sudden change from the dim light from which she had just emerged caused a sharp pain in her eyes. Before long, however, she became accustomed to the bright light, and looked about her.

A little fat, jolly-looking gnome, with a gold crown on his head, sat at a table, eating with great enjoyment from a steaming dish that was before him.

"Ah!" said the king, "whom have we here?
And what may be thy wish, my dear?"

King Rondo looked so extremely good-natured and plump and rosy that Wassa was not at all awed by his gold crown, and she answered readily:—

"I came to see the beautiful things that

Mona, the hunter's maid, told me about, and to take home with me some of those shining stones and pretty flowers."

"Where Mona went, thou too shalt go;
　The self-same paths to thee we'll show,"

answered the king as plainly as he could considering the large mouthful of "grubs on toast" that he was eating. Then, raising his voice, he called out: —

> "Will-o'-the-wisp, we bid thee bear
> Through all our paths this maiden fair.
> And, maiden, this fact know thou well,
> O'er all things here is fairy spell,
> And everything reflects, thou'lt see,
> The good or bad that dwells in thee.
> Then take with thee what thou lik'st most,
> While I return to grubs on toast."

Thus saying, the king resumed his repast with great relish, and Wassa looked about her for the guide whom the king had ordered to attend her. Lightly bounding toward her, and swinging his lantern gayly, came a Will-o'-the-wisp whom Wassa had often seen floating over the meadows, and whom she had vainly tried to overtake.

> "Come on, come on, no time to waste,
> So follow me as best thou mayst,"

called out the wisp, as he darted into one of the passages that led from the king's banquet hall.

"First of all," said Wassa, "show me the

grotto where the gold and silver fishes are; and thou must not go so fast, for thy lantern gives but little light."

The Will-o'-the-wisp darted down a narrow passageway, followed by Wassa, who found it difficult to keep closely to him, on account of the uneven ground. Soon, entering a large cave, the wisp suddenly stopped and swung his lantern over a dark pool. The little maid bent forward and gazed eagerly into the turbid water, but started back with an expression of disgust as she descried the ugly forms of reptiles wiggling through the dark stream.

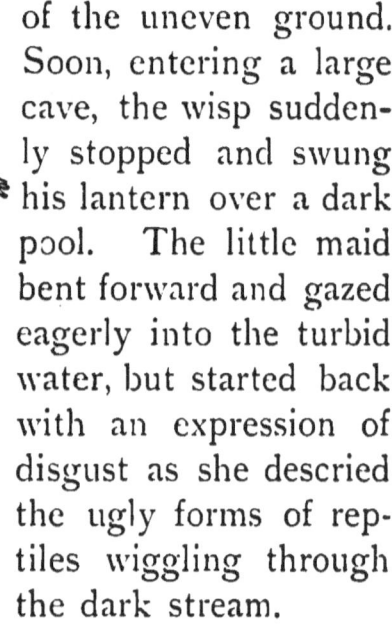

"I want to see the pretty gold and silver fishes, not these horrid creatures," exclaimed Wassa angrily. "Take me to them directly."

"All things in Fairyland, thou'lt find,
Reflect the colors of the mind,"

repeated the same voice Wassa had heard on her entrance.

"Where are the bright stones and flowers the fairies gave to Mona?" asked Wassa. "The king said I should take with me what I liked most, and I want those most."

> "Come," said the wisp, "and thou wilt find
> The things that most do suit thy mind."

And the wisp, swinging his lantern about his head, darted into another dark and narrow passageway.

"Where are the fairies who threw the pretty stones and flowers to Mona?" asked Wassa.

> "Look, maiden fair, and thou shalt see
> How fairies shower their gifts on thee,"

was heard from the same voice that had spoken before.

At these words Wassa felt a shower of stones falling over her shoulders, and glancing up, she shuddered as she beheld a grotesque face peering down at her. She clutched a handful of the stones, however, for even in that dim light they sparkled brilliantly.

"The grove with the beautiful plants and

singing birds,—thou must take me there," said Wassa.

> "Come," said the wisp, "and thou wilt find
> The things that most do suit thy mind,"

and he bounded on, until he paused, and, holding his lantern aloft, its rays fell on the sides of a grotto where beautiful trailing plants

were seen hanging, and waving palms brushed their large, broad leaves against Wassa's cheeks.

"This," said Wassa to herself, "does really seem like the grotto where the beautiful birds sang such sweet songs, but where are the birds?"

At that moment a harsh, discordant note startled the child, and a large bird with a hideous face and long bill flew close to her, then another, and still another, until the grotto resounded with their harsh notes.

"What can this mean?" thought Wassa. "Mona has purposely deceived me, but she shall answer for it to me."

Eager to escape from the noisy birds, Wassa begged the wisp to take her away, and she felt greatly relieved when she found herself safely out of the grotto. Through long and tedious passages they went, where hideously grinning faces appeared at every turn, and sometimes flowers and bright stones were showered upon her. Of these she secured as many as she could.

Wassa was very tired of Fairyland, and she began to doubt if she really were in that place. She suspected that the whole adventure might be an unpleasant dream, and she implored the Will-o'-the-wisp to conduct her to the open air.

> "Wouldst give to her of good things aught,
> Who, goaded on by jealous thought,
> From her home her friend entices
> By her false words and false devices?"

asked the voice she had heard before.

Still the wisp bounded gayly on, swinging his little lantern as merrily as before, and Wassa had no choice but to follow. The mischievous sprite always managed to keep his light from shining on the stones that lay in the path, and many a tumble the poor little maid had. Sometimes she splashed through a stream that she had not seen in the darkness, and at every mishap the shrill, mischievous laughter of unseen gnomes greeted her ears and made her misfortune all the harder to bear.

At last the wisp came to a standstill, and threw the light from his lantern upon a rocky wall that rose high above them. As it rolled slowly back on its hinges, the well-known voice chanted : —

> "Adieu, adieu, we'll see thee yet,
> Before another sun has set.
> And here thou'lt stay till thou shalt be
> Cured of the sin of jealousy."

Wassa did not trouble herself to discover the meaning of these ominous words, for there was the blue sky above her and the sunlight about her, and with a shout of joy she bounded through the open door and found herself at the foot of Blue Hill. Then she knew that she must have gone through the hill by underground passages.

Vainly did Wassa try to discover the door through which she had made her exit from Fairyland, and after a fruitless search she turned her steps homeward. Soon she bethought herself of the stones and flowers she had brought away with her, but imagine her disappointment and surprise at finding the stones merely dull pebbles, and the flowers withered and odorless.

"This is thy fault, Mona, and thou shalt pay for it," said Wassa aloud. "Thou hast deceived me very meanly;" and she set her mind at work to discover the best means of revenge.

Wassa had thought herself alone, but her vow of vengeance had been heard by the blue dragon-fly and the brown beetle, and as soon as she was out of sight, the dragon-fly gave vent to her indignation.

"Pay for it," she echoed; "we'll see about that, my little maid!"

The brown beetle watched the blue dragon-fly as she flew wildly round muttering angrily to herself. The gnats kept at a safe distance, for they knew well the temper of their queen.

"Well! what dost thou think about it? Hast thou no opinion on the subject?" asked the blue dragon-fly snappishly, suddenly addressing the brown beetle.

"Dear me!" replied the brown beetle, quite flustered at the suddenness of the remark, "I hardly know what to think. It serves her rightly, doesn't it?"

"Serves her rightly?" echoed the blue dragon-fly angrily; "what on earth dost thou mean?"

"For being so envious, thou know'st," replied the brown beetle humbly.

"Good gracious!" cried the blue dragon-fly, "if he doesn't think I was referring to that disagreeable girl going through Rondo's domain's! Of course it served her rightly! What I meant is, what dost thou think of Wassa's vow to revenge herself on the hunter's little maid for what she imagines she did?"

"Oh!" replied the beetle, "that is it, is it? Well, it would be a pity, would it not?"

"I should say so indeed!" replied the blue dragon-fly. "Hast thou nothing farther to say? Canst thou look on and see some mischievous trick played upon the innocent Mona, and not prevent it?"

"But how can I prevent it?" asked the brown beetle mildly.

"*I* can and will," replied the blue dragon-fly with energy. "A splendid idea has just this moment occurred to me."

The brown beetle dared not ask what the new idea was, and the blue dragon-fly didn't see fit to tell him, but she continued:—

"Those tiresome gnomes have some plan in their heads that concerns Wassa, but what it is nobody knows except themselves, unless it is the elves, and they will not tell. However, I intend to take the matter into my own hands. Dost thou happen to know where William of the wisp is?"

"Thou know'st he never comes out except at night," replied the brown beetle. "He is probably sleeping now."

"I know he is the most careless fellow in the world. He sleeps through the beautiful bright day, and comes out at night when he has to carry a lantern to see his way."

"Thou wilt see him as soon as it grows dark," said the beetle. " Every night I see him dancing about over the meadows. I know him by the little lantern he carries. Hast thou not seen him?"

"How can I see him when I never go out at night?" replied the blue dragon-fly in an irritable tone.

"I shall be glad to take thy message to him," replied the brown beetle politely.

"Thou!" exclaimed the dragon-fly rudely. "Thou wilt be sure to get things muddled in thy dull brain."

"Then I can send him to thee, and thou canst talk to him thyself," answered the brown beetle mildly.

"Thank thee," said the blue dragon-fly, her ill humor disappearing before the brown beetle's good nature, "thou art very kind. Tell him he will find me in the usual place by the yellow lily that grows just under the large maple in the meadow below."

The brown beetle promised to give the message correctly to the Will-o'-the-wisp, and away flew the giddy dragon-fly to sport in the bright sunlight, her attendants, as usual, following at a respectful distance.

When night came, the brown beetle, true to

his promise, cast his honest little eyes about in search of the Will-o'-the-wisp, and before long espied him dancing over the meadows, lighting up with his lantern the dark places over which he passed. It was not an easy task for the brown beetle with his slow gait to arrest the attention of the roving wisp, but at last he succeeded in doing so, and gave him the blue dragon-fly's message.

> "To the fair queen at once I'll speed,
> And see of what she is in need,"

replied the wisp, darting away in the direction indicated by the brown beetle.

CHAPTER IX.

THE BROWN BEETLE UNDERTAKES A MISSION

The brown beetle followed the Will-o'-the-wisp as fast as he could, sometimes flying and sometimes crawling; but his body was heavy and his wings were short, and the light wisp was soon out of sight. The beetle, however, persevered, and after a laborious journey, succeeded in reaching the large maple tree in the meadow, just in time to hear the closing words of the interview.

As the brown beetle stopped in front of the maple tree, the blue dragon-fly, poised on the edge of the yellow lily in which she made her home, was saying to the Will-o'-the-wisp: —

"The *softest* part of the cranberry bog, remember, where the water is deepest. Lead her well in."

The wisp, as he floated away, answered: —

> "Where the meadow's soft and wet,
> She'll be ere morrow's sun has set."

"Who'll be?" asked the brown beetle to himself. "Some mischief is planned, and it is evident they do not wish me to know what it is. I will stay in the meadow all day to-morrow, and find out what is going on. I hope they are not planning to injure the hunter's maid! No, certainly it cannot be she, for every one loves her. Now I remember that the blue dragon-fly was very indignant with the rover's maid, Wassa, but it would be too bad to play a mean trick upon her, if she *is* unkind to Mona without reason. If she is envious of her, — and she certainly is, — the unkind thoughts in her breast will cause her more trouble than she can cause Mona. Yes, I will be on the watch, and see if I can prevent the mischief."

The blue dragon-fly did not see the brown beetle, and as soon as the wisp had departed, she settled herself for a good long nap, so the brown beetle retreated as noiselessly as he had approached, and was soon fast asleep, himself, under a fine large oak leaf.

The day after her visit to Fairyland found Wassa in a very uncomfortable state of mind. Taking her brother and sisters into a secluded spot in the woods, she narrated her adventures of the day before, and expressed her opinion that Mona had purposely deceived her in describing the beauties of Fairyland.

"But her stones were bright, and her flowers as fresh as if they had just been plucked; and thy stones were dingy, and thy flowers withered," remarked the little lad.

This had the effect of making Wassa still more angry with Mona for having fared so much better than she had, and, like all envious dispositions, instead of venting her anger on those who were the cause of her disappointment, she made innocent Mona the one responsible for all her troubles.

"I know what I'll do," said Wassa after a pause. "I will entice her down into the meadows where the cranberries grow. I will tell her they are ripe, and she will get into the soft mud, and will have to stay there all night."

"That will be just right for her," replied the brother; "let us go now and find her."

"No," said Wassa, "it is too early in the day. Her father or mother would be sure to find her before night, and I intend to have her stay there in the dark and be well frightened."

Thus did Wassa's envious mind tempt her to plan a second mishap for Mona, and, as is always the case, the second piece of mischief was worse than the first.

"Oh! dost thou see that beautiful blue dragon-fly, Wassa?" cried the little sisters. "Do try to catch it for us."

"I believe it is the very same one I followed so far yesterday," replied Wassa. "It is of no use to try to catch it;" and, as she spoke, the blue dragon-fly soared high into the air, and flew rapidly away.

It was indeed the same dragon-fly that had enticed Wassa up Blue Hill the day before, and the dragon-fly had now followed the children and heard every word of Wassa's naughty plot.

"Now that I have everything arranged for carrying out my plan," said the blue dragon-fly to herself as she flew along, "I need have no further uneasiness. Will knows his *rôle*, and loves mischief enough to do it well. I wish to bathe," said the haughty queen, signalling to her attendants. "Find me a bath."

The willing maids in waiting at once conducted their queen to a small pool near by. The sun shone brightly down upon it, and lily pads floated on its clear surface, as if designed for resting places for just such airy creatures as the light dragon-fly. On the edge of the pool grew delicate water plants, and beyond them, on the moist banks, the scarlet cardinal flowers and fleur-de-lis, and as a background for all rose the tall forest trees.

"Gracious queen, we chose this secluded spot for your majesty's noonday bath," said the first lady in waiting in a respectful tone.

The haughty queen made no reply, but lightly skimmed over the pool, dipping the ends of her gauzy wings into the clear water, and shaking the shining drops over her. When tired of exercise, she rested for a moment on one of the lily pads, and then resumed her sport.

When the bath was completed, the dragon-fly summoned her gnats, who had been patiently waiting in the hot sun.

"Attend to my toilet," commanded the imperious queen.

At this began the work of beautifying the lovely queen. They carefully unfolded the gauzy wings, that had become wet in the bath, and spread them to their fullest expanse, that they might dry evenly in the hot sun; but to the first lady in waiting was given the care of the delicate face. Daintily must she dry the large and expressive eyes, of which the queen was so proud; and she alone knew how to powder the royal countenance with the pollen of the fairest flowers.

In due time the queen's toilet was completed and her majesty pronounced faultlessly adorned. Flying over the clearest part of the pool, she glanced down at the image reflected there, and surely the most exacting mistress could not have failed to be satisfied with the work of her handmaidens. Never were dragon-fly's wings gauzier or smoother. The beautiful blue of her slender body actually glistened in the sunshine, and the fragrant powder imparted a bloom to her expressive countenance.

Giving a little nod of approval as reward to her patient attendants, away flew the haughty queen to disport herself in the warm sunshine, followed by her ladies in waiting, who held themselves in readiness to be summoned at any moment.

All day long Wassa was in a state of uneasiness. She watched from a distance the form of the hunter's little maid as the bright cap and neat dress of skins flitted among the trees, or attended to the flowers in the little garden. Not until the sun was down did Wassa attempt to carry out her plan; but when twilight with its soft shadows appeared, she set out in the direction of the hunter's cabin.

Before Wassa had taken many steps, however, there sprang from behind a tall clump of bushes the Will-o'-the-wisp, swinging his little lantern, and singing gayly:—

"Follow, follow where I go,
Whoever would my secret know."

At sight of the mischievous sprite who had led her through the dark and unpleasant paths in Fairyland, Wassa at once forgot the object she had in view. The annoying experience of the day before rose vividly before her mind, and she resolved to overtake and punish the mischievous imp who had caused her so many falls and bruises.

"I'll follow thee, be sure of that," cried Wassa angrily, "and what is more, I'll overtake thee too. In the dark passages of Fairyland thou hadst it all thy own way, but here, in the woods, I know every step of the way, and if I cannot overtake thee, mite that thou art, it would be a pity."

A mocking laugh from the wisp was the only reply, and at that the chase began in earnest. Away went the wisp, followed closely by the excited Wassa. Over stones and stumps and bushes bounded the light Will-o'-the-wisp, and, in spite of Wassa's vigorous exertions, he managed to keep the distance between them exactly the same.

Faster and faster came Wassa's breath, but so lightly did the wisp float along that he remained as fresh as when he first started.

> "O'er bush and o'er stone, when the day's done,
> The chase is ended, the race is won,"

called out the wisp.

Wassa now noticed for the first time that the day was nearly done, but this only caused her to redouble her efforts, and on they went, faster than ever. She did not observe that the wary wisp drew her farther and farther into the woods, and nearer to the very meadow into which she had intended to entice the hunter's little maid.

As he approached the meadow, the wisp occasionally allowed his pursuer to approach so closely that she could almost put her hand on him, and then, at the very moment she thought to grasp him, off he was again, as distant as before. This had the effect of making Wassa more determined to succeed, and she redoubled her speed, not heeding in her excitement that the ground under her feet was becoming damp and soft.

At last it seemed as if the strength of the wisp were indeed giving out. He was almost within Wassa's grasp, his steps wavered, and the light from his lantern flickered and grew dim. Wassa made a vigorous bound forward, with both hands extended, when suddenly the apparently exhausted wisp gave a long leap to one side, out went the lantern, and Wassa plunged heavily forward, up to her knees in water, and felt her feet gradually settling in the soft mud of the cranberry bog, — the very spot into which she had intended to entice innocent Mona.

"Help!" screamed Wassa, striving vainly to extricate herself, "help! I am sinking deeper and deeper in the mire!"

"The chase is o'er, the race is won,
There wilt thou stay till rise of sun.
Thou mad'st thy plan, and so did we,
But we planned best, as thou dost see,"

called out the mischievous wisp, suddenly appearing with his lantern lighted.

To Wassa's plaintive calls for help the wisp replied only with jeering laughs and derisive questions, and, after satisfying his merriment, left her to her fate. She watched him as long as he was in sight, as he danced over the meadow and finally disappeared from her view.

Loudly and long did Wassa cry for help, but not a sound reached her in reply, except the lonesome cries of the night birds and the occasional barking of foxes.

"Get away, thou horrid thing!" exclaimed Wassa angrily as a large brown beetle flew against her.

The beetle was none other than our honest little friend, who, convinced that mischief was intended, had set his dull little mind to work to discover what was going on about him.

A conscientious soul as ever lived was the brown beetle, and, in spite of Wassa's rude repulse, he was determined to assist her in her trouble if he could. But what could he do? He set his slow mind to work. This mischief he was sure was the result of the conversation between the blue dragon-fly and the Will-o'-the-wisp, and neither of them was conscientious enough to repair the harm done.

Meanwhile Wassa's cries still continued, but not a plan for her rescue could the beetle devise. Suddenly he bethought himself of the spirit of the dell. She was so powerful, might she not be able to assist him?

No sooner did this thought take form in the brown beetle's mind than he set off at once, tired although he was, to seek an interview with the spirit of the dell.

Through the dark, wet meadow flew and crawled the good little beetle, bent on his errand of mercy, often stopping to rest.

"Good Will-o'-the-wisp, wilt thou not light me on my way? The night is very dark," called out the beetle.

But the selfish and waggish wisp refused to aid the beetle, and he continued his journey alone.

At last the beetle met a glowworm, wriggling his shining body through the meadow grass, and he begged him to lend him his light; but the glowworm refused when he was told for whom his assistance was needed.

"If it were to help the hunter's little maid, I would willingly assist thee," replied the glowworm, "but I will not loan my light for Wassa.

She has destroyed too many of our tribe for that."

With a sigh of despair, on went the good little beetle, until he met a large firefly skimming lightly along.

"Good firefly, wilt thou not lend me thy light to find the spirit of the dell? I seek her aid to free a poor little maid who is fast in yon cranberry bog."

"What may be the name of the little maid?" asked the firefly, stopping for an instant.

"She is called Wassa," replied the brown beetle.

"Not I!" replied the firefly. "Wassa has chased me too many times for that; and too many of our tribe have been captured by her. If it were the hunter's little maid I would willingly go with thee."

"Shall I ever reach the spirit of the dell?" murmured the good little beetle as the firefly soared high into the air. "None will help me."

At last the beetle bethought himself of the moon.

"Dear, good moon," pleaded the patient little beetle, "wilt thou not light me on my way to the spirit of the dell? I know Wassa is not a good, kind child, but she is in a sad plight, and it seems wrong not to try to assist her. Do, I pray thee, lend me a little of thy light. It is so very dark."

Almost before the beetle finished, out came the moon from behind a cloud, full and bright, and lighted up the meadow from end to end. A placid, motherly smile was on her face, and the good little beetle's heart gave a great leap for joy.

Now the way was as clear as if it were daylight, and with his little heart beating with courage and hope, the brown beetle soon reached the river in which the spirit of the dell made her home.

CHAPTER X.

THE LAND OF THE AFTER-GLOW.

The river looked very wide and long to the brown beetle, and he never before, in the course of his life, had felt so small and helpless. He was sorely tempted to abandon his intention of summoning the spirit of the dell, but as he hesitated, a faint cry for help from Wassa in the distant cranberry bog determined him.

With his heart beating loudly against his little sides, the brown beetle recited the lines which he knew would summon the powerful spirit of the dell:—

> "Spirit of the dell so fair,
> List, I pray, unto my prayer.
> Dull am I, but wise art thou;
> Wilt thou deign to tell me how
> I can rescue from her plight
> That poor maid, ere morning's light?"

For a moment there was silence, during which the beetle's heart thumped more loudly than ever. Then a faint streak of mist was seen rising on the distant river. Nearer and nearer it came, very distinct in the bright moonlight, until it stood opposite to the brown beetle, when it remained stationary.

Gradually the column of mist assumed the form of a beautiful female figure, and slowly and gracefully it bent toward the brown beetle, until these words, that sounded like the wind breathing softly through the forest pines, fell on the beetle's ears:—

"From the land of mist and dew
 Come I when one calls on me.
Tell me, beetle good and true,
 If I can do aught for thee."

The dull mind of the good little beetle felt a glow of pleasure at this kind reception. Slow of speech was he, but he knew it was proper to address the spirit of the dell in the language usually spoken by the fairy-folk, so with a great effort he answered as well as he was able: —

> "Gracious spirit of the dell,
> Wassa is in direful need.
> Grant to me a fairy spell
> That shall rescue her with speed."

For answer, the spirit of the dell slowly moved her head from side to side as she answered: —

> "Spell was never wove by me,
> Nor either potent charm I own
> That can set poor Wassa free;
> So adieu, good beetle brown."

"Oh! dear," cried the beetle in his native tongue as the spirit of the dell receded and her form grew fainter and fainter, "pray tell me what to do! I cannot leave that poor maid in such a plight, and I am too small and stupid to rescue her myself. It must be that some one has power to help me. Only tell me where to find him, and I will go as long as I can move my wings."

Still slowly receding, the spirit replied:—

> "Who has courage, beetle brown,
> And a kind heart, then he may
> To the After-glow go down,
> And seek the little man in gray."

As the spirit of the dell spoke the last words, merely a column of mist was seen in the distance, and in a moment more that too was gone.

"What shall I do? How can I ever find him?" moaned the poor little beetle.

"Whoo! Whoo!" shouted a large owl close at hand.

"Why, the little man in gray," replied the brown beetle. "The spirit of the dell told me to seek him in the land of the After-glow. Canst thou tell me where it is?"

"Never heard of the place," said the owl. "But I know who can tell thee, if there really is such a place, which I very much doubt."

"Oh! tell me," cried the brown beetle quickly, "who can direct me?"

"My cousin, Judge Owl," replied the owl. "He is very wise, and knows by heart all the 'Laws of the Woods.'"

"Where can I find him?" asked the brown beetle.

"By the two large chestnut trees in yonder wood," answered the owl.

"Then the sooner I start on my journey the better," said the brown beetle, "for I go but slowly, and the night is already far gone. I would that my wings were as long and strong as thine;" and the patient little beetle sighed as he glanced admiringly at the strong wings of his companion.

"Sit on my back and thou wilt soon be there," said the owl obligingly.

The brown beetle hastened to take advantage of this kind offer, and they were soon rushing through the air at a speed that quite took away the beetle's breath. They were soon over the spot where the two large chestnuts stood, and the owl descended in graceful circles, and alighted on a branch of the largest tree.

Seated in solemn dignity in a crotch of the

huge tree was Judge Owl, the wisest and most experienced of birds. As he turned his great yellow eyes upon the brown beetle, that modest little creature felt that he had indeed taken a great liberty in presenting himself before such a powerful personage.

"What is thy business?" demanded the judge in solemn tones, after he had stared so long at the brown beetle that the poor little creature was frightened out of his wits.

"Wilt thou be kind enough to tell me if it says in the 'Laws of the Woods' where the land of the After-glow lies?" said the little beetle timidly.

"What hast thou to do with the land of the After-glow, pray?" asked the judge sternly.

"The little man in gray dwells there," replied the brown beetle meekly.

"Dost thou mean to say that thou hast the audacity to seek the little gray man?" asked Judge Owl.

"The spirit of the dell told me to go to him," answered the brown beetle; and he related how Wassa had been decoyed into the cranberry bog by the mischievous Will-o'-the-wisp, and expressed his determination to obtain aid for her.

"Will is a tricky fellow," said the judge. "I wonder the little maid did not know better than to follow him. Thou art brave and good-natured, beetle, and I will try to help thee;" and the judge's countenance grew quite mild as he gazed at the little beetle.

Judge Owl sat for a few moments lost in thought, with one eye closed and the other wide open. He could think much better thus, and it gave him a look of great wisdom. The little brown beetle himself was greatly awed by it.

"Ha! I have it!" exclaimed the judge after a long pause, and he repeated solemnly these lines: —

> "Let all men by these presents know,
> That the land of the After-glow
> Sends back from the hill so blue
> Rosy rays of the sunset hue."

"Now," said Judge Owl, when he had finished, and in his most pompous manner, "what is clearer than that?"

"Very clear indeed, and I thank thee with all my heart," replied the brown beetle gratefully. "It was very stupid of me not to think of it before."

"If all were wise, my little friend, there would be no occasion for the 'Laws of the Woods.' We have them to straighten out matters," answered Judge Owl.

"There is no time to lose," said the owl who had so obligingly conducted the brown beetle thither, "and if thou sayest so, I will take thee to the land of the After-glow."

"With all my heart," replied the brown beetle, and, tightly clutching the owl's thick feathers with his prickly little feet, they were once more soaring through the air at a rapid flight.

On his expedition went the brown beetle, sailing high over the tallest trees and brooks and meadows, the moon shining steadily and patiently to light him on his way, until the owl alighted on a tree that grew on the western side of the Blue Hill.

"Now, good little beetle, I can do no more for thee. I must do much work before daylight. But I wish thee all success;" and away flew the owl without waiting for thanks.

The brown beetle found himself alone on the great hill. Not a living creature was in sight, and the beetle felt smaller and more powerless than ever. The placid face of the moon seemed to encourage him, and, taking heart, in a faint voice he called on the little gray man thus: —

> "O most mighty man in gray,
> Listen to my call, I pray.
> Almost, now, the night is gone,
> And my work is left undone.
> Thou alone canst do the deed;
> Wilt thou not my summons heed?"

All was still as before; not a rustle of leaf or twig broke the profound silence that followed the brown beetle's appeal; but he gave a great start of surprise as the little gray man stood suddenly before him.

"Thou hast summoned me, little brown beetle; what is it thou wouldst have me do?" asked the little gray man.

"O mighty man in gray," cried the brown beetle, "the rover's little maid is fast in the cold, wet cranberry bog, calling vainly for help. Wilt thou not rescue her?"

"Why dost thou concern thyself about that little maid?" asked the little gray man, looking intently, but not unkindly, on the brown beetle.

"Because I cannot hear her piteous cries without wishing to help her," replied the beetle.

"Dost thou not know the naughty pranks her envy of the hunter's little maid has led her to commit?" asked the little gray man.

"I know them all," replied the beetle sadly.

"And did she not repulse thee rudely but now?"

"It is true," answered the beetle.

"And still thou hast undertaken for her an arduous and dangerous task," said the little gray man in a kindly tone. "Little beetle, thou hast a large heart beneath thy honest brown skin, and for thy sake will I grant thy request. Go to thy rest, good beetle, and I will finish thy task."

The little gray man lightly stamped his foot upon the rock upon which he stood. Soon a rumbling was heard, and the ground vibrated as if swayed by an earthquake. The brown beetle understood what this meant, and watched from his safe position on a hazel bush to see what was about to happen.

Before long, huge objects were seen coming down the hill, one after another. These the beetle knew were the giants; and, as they approached, they rubbed their sleepy eyes, and stretched their long legs with many a yawn that reverberated among the hills like claps of thunder.

"Here we are, master," said the giants as they halted before the little gray man. "What wouldst thou with us?"

"Wake up, ye great sleepy heads, and listen to me," said the little gray man sternly, as an unusually loud yawn was heard.

"We try, master," answered one of the giants, "but we sleep soundly, and it is not easy to shake off sleep at so short a notice."

The little gray man continued in a milder tone: —

"The rover's little maid is imprisoned in yonder cranberry bog, and must be rescued this night."

"There let her stay," answered one of the giants roughly; "it will be a lesson for her. We have heard of her plottings against the hunter's little maid. There let her stay, I say."

"What!" cried the little gray man in the imperious tone that always subdued the giants, "wouldst thou rebel against my authority?"

"Master, forgive," replied the giant submissively; "I meant not to dispute thy commands. But we know this little maid to be envious-minded, and we would unwillingly assist her."

"Listen to me," commanded the little man,

"and question not my orders. Yonder pebble," pointing to a spur of the hill that broke its even outline, "lies in our path. Do thou, Rockroller, pick it up and cast it into the ocean."

Rockroller approached the mass of rock, and placing his hands under its edges, bent to the task of disengaging it from its solid foundation. The sinews of his brawny arms swelled and knotted with the gigantic effort. One more vigorous pull, and yet another, and slowly the huge mass gave way. Then taking it firmly in the hollow of his great hand, and steadying himself for the task, with his feet wide apart, giant Rockroller gave his strong right arm a mighty swing, and away sped the huge mass far over the hill, growing smaller and smaller, until it looked like a speck in the distance, then gradually disappeared behind a wooded hill. Immediately a shower of foam arose as it splashed into the ocean, and there it stands to this day, and is known by the name of "Half Tide Rock."

"Twigtwister, come hither," commanded the little gray man, and the great giant came forward.

"Dost thou see yonder grove of saplings?" asked the little gray man, pointing to a forest of lofty pines that lay between the hill and the cranberry bog.

"Aye, master," answered the giant meekly.

"Pull them up, Twigtwister; they will serve to light thy fire for to-morrow's meal," said the little gray man.

Twigtwister stepped up to the forest, and, stooping over one of the tallest pines, grasped it with both hands, and with all his strength, as a child would uproot a weed, twisted it from side to side. Slowly the earth about the huge tree loosened, and fissures appeared above the long roots. Still the giant twisted, and soon the large roots appeared above the ground. Gradually the giant straightened his tall form, and, as he stood upright, he held in his hand the great tree with its trailing roots.

One after another of the huge pines did Twigtwister uproot, until not one was left, and a great pile of trees and roots towered beside him.

"A goodly handful of twigs hast thou for thy fire," remarked the little gray man.

"Swiftstepper," commanded once more the little gray man, "come hither."

"Here, master," answered that giant as he came forward.

"Step over to yon cranberry bog and bring to me the little maid thou wilt find there; and mind thou play'st no tricks with me," said the little gray man.

"Aye, master; to hear is to obey," answered Swiftstepper; and, striding over the forest as easily as a man would walk over a grassy field, his first step carried him half a mile; the next step took him beyond the range of the smaller hills, and with the next one he was out of sight.

In a few moments the giant reappeared, the same gigantic strides bringing him to the spot where the little gray man stood, and the struggling Wassa was placed before the little man in gray.

CHAPTER XI.

WASSA RETURNS TO FAIRYLAND.

You may be sure that Wassa was well frightened when she found herself before the little gray man and saw all the huge giants about her, but even that was preferable to remaining all night in the cold, wet cranberry bog.

The giant Swiftstepper had placed Wassa directly in front of the little man in gray, and she could but look at him. His countenance was very stern.

"Wassa," began the little man in gray, "thou art well known to me. All the mischief thy envy of the hunter's little maid has caused thee to do I know. Thou it was who took from her nets the fishes, and my little elves, not she, put the stones in thy net. Thou, too, it was who sought to hide the net at the bottom of the pond, and thou again it was who enticed the little maid up the hill, and tossed her pretty cap where thou thought'st it never again would be found; but the fairy-folk watch over all kindly souls, and again was thy intended mischief prevented, and good came from thy evil intentions, for by that means was Mona enabled to see the beauties of Fairyland. I know, too, what thou hadst planned to do this very night; and, had it not been for the honest little friend that pleaded thy cause, I would have left thee sticking in the cranberry bog, as thou didst plan to leave Mona."

"Mona is proud of her fine clothes, and it would have served her right to lose her fine cap," said Wassa sulkily.

"She likes the cap as thou wouldst like it if it were thine, because it is pretty, and also because it is a gift from her mother," replied the little man.

"She is a spoiled child," said Wassa.

"The worst kind of spoiled children are those who envy others for having what they themselves have not," said the little gray man severely. "I perceive, my little maid, that thy heart is still full of envy, and that thou wilt make thy younger brother and sisters as envious as thou art. Therefore this have I decided to do: thou shalt be placed in charge of my little gnomes, and have the care of a truly spoiled child until thou hast learned to know thy own heart. Swiftstepper, take up this little maid once more and bear her to King Rondo's domains. He knows what he has to do."

With these words the little man in gray vanished as suddenly as he had appeared; and, in spite of her struggles, Swiftstepper once more picked up Wassa, and, with one of his long strides, stood before the high stone wall that shut in King Rondo's domains.

The huge door rolled slowly back, the giant placed Wassa inside, then withdrew, and the door rolled back into place.

While Wassa was imprisoned in the cranberry bog, the elves, as was their nightly custom, assembled for their revels. This night they were unusually gay and noisy, and peals of laughter were heard continually.

Since several days the elves had been putting their little heads together and plotting with their little brains, and now, at last, their plans were perfected. In their midst stood that mischief-loving sprite, Toto the Slim. Whatever he had been saying afforded his companions great amusement, for they were actually holding their little sides from laughter, and the blue dragon-fly, asleep in the yellow lily, awoke in time to catch these words from Toto:—

> "My friends, it is too bad, ye know,
> But I fear it will have to go."

Then with a dapper air Toto the Slim twirled the ends of his blond mustache, that was as light as thistle down, and of about the same shade, and that was the hope and pride of his life. Was it possible he meant that *that* must go? The blue dragon-fly could hardly believe it, and *why* must it go?

Toto knelt by the brink of the pond, and, using its clear surface for a mirror, and a piece of sharp-edged grass for a razor, with a few quick, skilful strokes, off came his beloved mustache.

What a change was wrought in him! Could it be Toto the Slim? He was fair and plump and rosy, looking like a dimpled child of three.

"Think ye," he cried, as he gayly laughed, "that I could pass for a spoiled child?"

And Toto, puckering up his rosy little mouth, imitated the crying of a naughty, peevish child, at the same time jumping up and down and stamping his feet after the manner of spoiled children.

The blue dragon-fly wondered more and more at this conduct of Toto's. Why did he want to pass for a spoiled child? While she was busied in wondering, a gnome appeared, and hastily informed Toto the Slim that King Rondo wished him to hasten to the cavern as Wassa was already there.

At this summons away sped Toto the Slim, followed by the band of elves, and also by the blue dragon-fly, who was curious to fathom the mystery. When they reached the cave the rocky door rolled back, and Toto the slim nimbly slipped inside. The door fell back into its place, and the dragon-fly was no wiser than before.

Wassa found herself surrounded by gnomes, who, crowding about her, hurried her into the banquet hall where King Rondo sat eating his evening meal. As Wassa entered, he finished his repast, and, pushing back his seat, beckoned to his gnomes to bring Wassa to him.

It was impossible for King Rondo to make his fat rosy face look otherwise than jolly and good-humored, particularly just after a hearty meal of his favorite dish of 'grubs on toast." The king, however, tried to look as stern as possible, and drew his hand over his face to give the lines a downward curve. When Wassa was placed before him he looked at her for a while in silence, to impress her with his dignity, and then addressed her thus: —

> "This time, my dear, thou'st come to stay,
> So says the little man in gray;
> And trials great must be endured
> Until of envy thou art cured.
> For there's no fault beneath the sun
> That does more harm than this same one.
> The best way is, to draw it mild,
> To be the nurse of a spoiled child.
> What ho there, gnomes! I pray thee bring
> The fairy prince before the king."

One of the gnomes quickly disappeared, and immediately were heard loud outcries like those made by self-willed children, and in a moment the gnome reappeared, bearing in his arms the fairy prince, who was screaming and struggling to free himself.

The king, frowning upon the gnome, said: —

> "Hey dey! hey dey! what is all this?
> And what is it that's gone amiss?"

"Sire, the young prince was hard at play,
And did not wish to come this way."
And all this time the naughty child
Filled the air with screams so wild.
"Prince," said the king, "listen to me;
Wassa has come thy nurse to be.
Her duty is to wait on thee,
And to thy whims she must agree."
Then turning to the maid he said,
"Go, put the prince at once to bed."

Not daring to disobey the king, Wassa went toward the prince and attempted to take him from the arms of the gnome, but the instant she put out her arms to take him, the prince gave vent to terrific howls, and kicked and struggled harder than ever.

"Thou horrid nurse, now go away!
I will not go with thee, I say!"

screamed the naughty prince.

Wassa looked toward the king, expecting him to interfere and compel his little son to do as he desired, but, to her surprise, he seemed well pleased with the prince's behavior, and laughed until his double chin shook.

"Let him, Wassa, have his way,
Thou must never say him nay,"

said the king, whereupon the fairy prince screamed louder than ever.

At last the king evidently became tired of listening to the child's screams, and ordered Wassa to pick up the prince and take him to bed, and Wassa endeavored to obey.

Not so minded was the fairy prince, however.

"To the fishes' cave, I say!
With them I wish awhile to play,"

commanded the prince, and Wassa dared not oppose him. So, taking him in her arms, she sought the cave, where, on her former visit, she had seen the ugly reptiles wriggling their way through the dark water. On that night the cave was dark, but now all Fairyland was ablaze with light. In the grotto the water of the pond was now clear as crystal, and gold and silver fishes sported through it, exactly as Mona had described it.

Wassa set the fairy prince on the ground, and he amused himself by reaching far over the edge of the pond and trying to catch the fishes as they swam by. This caused Wassa great uneasiness for fear he might tumble in, and she dreaded the consequences that would fol-

WASSA RETURNS TO FAIRYLAND. 151

low such carelessness on her part. She tried to hold her venturesome charge back, but at every attempt to restrain him he set up a yell that resounded through the cavern so loudly that Wassa feared it would reach the ears of the king.

The fairy prince continued this sport until Wassa was very weary, and she tried in vain to persuade him to allow her to take him to bed.

"No!" cried the prince, I tell thee no!
To the birds' cave I wish to go."

Nothing was to be done but to carry the obstreperous prince to the cave of the birds, and a weary walk it was, through long and brilliantly lighted passages. Often must Wassa stop for her charge to look at the bright stones that adorned the sides of the cavern, and to pick the gay flowers that grew in the path.

After a tedious walk, the cave of the birds was reached, but how different was it from what Wassa saw before! A light bright as the most brilliant sunshine streamed through the trees laden with the most tempting fruit and blossoms, and bright-plumaged birds sang melodiously among the branches.

Not one of the delicious fruits, however, could Wassa reach. The prince picked them at his pleasure, and ate of them with great relish, but the instant Wassa attempted to touch one, it vanished like magic from her hand.

For a while the prince entertained himself with the gay birds, and climbed at will over the lower branches of the trees, but, as in the cave of the fishes, he would not allow Wassa to touch him. Often she thought him about to fall headlong from a branch, but he screamed loudly if she attempted to put her hand on him, and always recovered himself in time to prevent a fall.

Wassa was now so weary that she could hardly keep her head erect, and she endeavored to persuade her wilful charge to go to bed, but he refused with loud cries.

"No, to the sea I'll go, I say,
With mermaids there I wish to play,"

cried the unreasonable prince.

"It is too late to go to the sea to-night," replied Wassa. "Go to bed now, sweet prince, and in the morning I will take thee to the sea."

The prince, however, insisted that he should not go to bed until he had been to the sea and played with the mermaids.

"But I do not know the way to the sea," replied Wassa; "it must be very far."

>"The brook goes to the sea, they say.
>My royal pa thou must obey,"

answered the naughty little prince.

"And must we follow the brook all that distance?" asked Wassa.

>"The fairy of the brook will know
>How to the mermaids we must go,"

replied the prince.

"But I do not know where to find the fairy of the brook," said Wassa, who had learned to believe most fully in fairies.

The prince bent over the brook that flowed quietly at their feet, and said:—

>"Fairy of this stream so fair,
>Wilt thou kindly tell me where,
>How far distant it may be
>To the waters of the sea?"

A veil of mist arose on the stream, and was wafted toward the fairy prince, until the delicate form of a fairy appeared within, and a low voice spoke thus: —

"Too long the way, too short the night,
 'Tis best to wait till morning's light.
 Then come to me and I will say
 A spell to send thee on thy way."

With these words the fairy of the brook gradually resolved into mist and floated down the stream.

"No!" bawled the prince, with all his might,
 "I'll go, I say, this very night."

"Thou canst not go," said Wassa. "The fairy of the brook said it was too late and too far to go there to-night. So come back with me like a good little prince, and I will take thee to the sea early in the morning."

"No!" screamed the prince, "I will go now, I'll *make* the fairy tell me how!"

Then the perverse little prince threw himself on the ground and renewed his screaming, until Wassa, finding entreaties of no avail, allowed him to scream and kick until he stopped from sheer exhaustion, when he fell fast asleep. Then Wassa picked him up, carried him home, and put him to bed; then, thoroughly weary herself, she was soon sleeping as soundly as her exacting charge.

CHAPTER XII.

THE FAIRY PRINCE AND THE MERMAIDS.

If Wassa had hoped that his night's sleep would cause the fairy prince to forget his purpose of visiting the mermaids, she was greatly mistaken, for as soon as his eyes opened the next morning he called loudly:—

> "O nurse, wake up! In yonder sea
> Those pretty mermaids wait for me."

"It is very early to start," pleaded Wassa, who had not slept half long enough, "and thou hast not had thy breakfast yet."

> "I don't want anything to eat,"
> He cried, and stamped with both his feet.
> "If thou art cross and bad to me,
> I'll send for pa, as thou wilt see."

Wassa knew that King Rondo could not be far off, and, remembering his command that she was to allow the fairy prince to have his own way in all things, there was nothing to be done but to allow the wilful prince to do as he wished, so, with a sigh of despair, she took him up and carried him to the spot where the night before the fairy of the brook had appeared to them.

Once more the prince repeated these lines:—

> "Fairy of the stream so fair,
> Wilt thou kindly tell me where,
> How far distant it may be
> To the waters of the sea?"

As before, the column of mist appeared in the distance and floated on the stream until it reached the prince, and the fairy of the brook from within the mist answered:—

> "Seldom is it, prince, that we
> Grant that mortals mermaids see.
> A wilful child must have its way,
> And we cannot say thee nay.
> But this mark well: let not a word
> Or cry, while on the way, be heard.
> If thou shouldst speak or cry, all's lost,
> And from the bark wouldst thou be tossed."

With these words, the form of the fairy of the brook was once more veiled in mist and receded down the stream.

THE FAIRY PRINCE AND THE MERMAIDS. 159

No sooner did the mist disappear than from the same spot where it vanished appeared a fairy boat that sailed rapidly toward the prince

and Wassa. The sail, which was spread wide, was made of butterflies' wings, and the brilliant light of Fairyland falling on them caused them to shine with rainbow hues. The shrouds were of the finest cobwebs, and the airy craft floated on the water like thistle down.

Silently the prince and Wassa stepped aboard the magic boat, and it bore them down the stream. After a while the stream grew broader and broader, and light waves rippled its surface, but the fairy bark glided lightly over them without any perceptible motion. Rapids, too, there were, down which the bark shot with hardly a tremor of its frail sides, and as they proceeded, a light, fresh breeze, fragrant with sea odors, was wafted toward them.

All this time the fairy prince had been quite silent, sitting with one hand hanging over the boat's side and dangling in the cool water; but before long the desire to dip both hands in seized the wilful prince, and he suddenly plunged the other hand in.

Thinking her venturesome charge would lose his balance and fall headlong into the water, Wassa suddenly seized him, and tried to draw him back, but with an angry scream the prince exclaimed:—

"Put both hands in I must and will,
Naughty Wassa, so keep still!"

No sooner were these words spoken than the fairy prince and Wassa found themselves on the bank of the stream, and the fairy bark nowhere to be seen.

"Now thou see'st," said Wassa, "what comes of thy naughtiness. Thou hast disobeyed the fairy of the brook, and thou canst not go to the sea."

> "I must and will go to the sea!
> So take me up and carry me!"

cried the naughty little prince.

Thus ordered, Wassa took up her wilful charge and walked along the brook side until her feet were very weary. At last they came in sight of the ocean, and as the fresh air fanned her cheeks, Wassa felt her courage revive, and hastened her steps.

"Now," said Wassa as she stood on the shore and set the prince on the shining sand, "what are we to do next? There are no mermaids here."

> "Far out at sea the mermaids stay,
> And there they sport the livelong day,"

replied the prince.

"One thing is certain, we cannot go to

them," said Wassa, "so thou must content thyself to play in this shining sand."

The fairy prince, however, had no intention of abandoning his project of visiting the mermaids, and looking far out into the ocean, he murmured: —

> "Monarch of the ocean wide
> And all that dwell within its tide,
> Wilt thou kindly take us where
> In its depths sport mermaids fair?"

The ocean became agitated, and small, white-capped waves broke against the sandy beach, and from the depths of the ocean a tiny figure appeared, wearing a golden crown and bearing in its hand a sceptre. Its garments were made of shining seaweed, and its golden crown and sceptre were studded with precious stones. In a voice that sounded like waves gently breaking on the shore, the monarch of the sea murmured: —

> "Prince, the boon thou ask'st of me
> Shall ere long be granted thee;
> But this thing know — if any word
> Of rage or spite from thee is heard,
> Where'er thou art, there shalt thou stay,
> Thou shalt not return this way."

With these words the monarch of the sea vanished beneath the waves, and the waters became quiet as before. Ere long a gleaming object in the distance was seen approaching, and as it came nearer it proved to be a fairy nautilus.

The nautilus glided up to the shore, and the two wanderers stepped within. Away glided the fairy craft toward the deep sea, leaving the shore farther and farther behind until it was no longer visible. No other craft was in sight, and the only living creatures to be seen were the sea-birds that occasionally dipped their long beaks into the water in search of prey, and the fishes that sometimes swam to the surface.

As the nautilus sailed farther out to sea, huge whales spouted about them, covering them with foam, and fierce-looking sharks darted by.

All these things the prince noted, as they sailed rapidly along, leaning over the side of the light bark; but as Wassa caught sight of an immense shark that followed in their wake, its cruel eyes fastened on the nautilus, she suddenly reached forward and drew the fairy prince farther back. With a cry of anger the prince exclaimed:—

"Let go, I say, and let me be!
The pretty fishes I want to see!"

Instantly the nautilus changed its course, and Wassa and the fairy prince found themselves on a small island in the midst of the ocean.

"Now see what thy naughtiness has again brought upon us!" exclaimed Wassa angrily. "Here, on this desert island, must we stay forever, just as the sea-monarch said."

"What do I care if here we stay?
With pretty mermaids I shall play,"

cried the spoiled child, and, stooping, he began to dabble in the clear water that rippled against the rocky edge of the island.

"There are no mermaids here," answered Wassa in a cross tone, "and I have heard enough of mermaids. Thy wilfulness has brought about a fine state of affairs!" and tears of vexation stood in her eyes.

"The mermaids come, I told thee so;
With them to play I mean to go,"

cried the prince gleefully, pointing to the distant ocean.

"Those are not mermaids," said Wassa; "it is but a school of dolphins. Besides, there are no such beings as mermaids, and it is very foolish for thee to persist in believing in them."

Wassa was not mistaken, for a large school of dolphins was approaching, and Wassa watched them with great interest, for they were evidently making directly for the island. Rolling and pitching about as they swam, the water foamed and surged about them, and sometimes they disappeared altogether beneath the surface, coming up each time much nearer to the island.

> "Dost thou not see the shining hair
> And golden combs of mermaids fair?"

cried the prince.

Wassa was thunderstruck to see a beautiful maiden seated on the back of each, as the dolphins came nearer. In one hand each held a mirror, the frame of which gleamed with gems and precious ore, and in the other hand a golden comb, with which she combed her shining tresses, which shone like the brilliant green seaweed that floats on the surface of the ocean.

THE FAIRY PRINCE AND THE MERMAIDS. 167

As the dolphins approached nearer to the island they disappeared beneath the surface of the water once more, and rose just at the feet of the fairy prince, the water falling in drops from the beautiful mermaidens like myriads of diamonds.

So engaged in watching the mermaids was Wassa, that for the moment she forgot her charge, until she saw him suddenly leap far into the water, and spring upon the back of a dolphin.

"O prince, come back to me!" cried

Wassa. "Thou canst not trust the mermaids. Oh! what will King Rondo say to me?" and she rung her hands in desperation.

The wilful prince, however, paid no attention to Wassa's entreaties, but sat his dolphin as if he had passed his life on its back, and the mermaidens smiled sweetly on him as they combed their shining locks.

"Perhaps," thought Wassa, as she saw the fairy prince so unconcerned, "he has done this thing before, and when he becomes tired of the sport he will come back of his own accord. One thing is certain: the more I entreat him to return, the longer he will stay away, he is so perverse."

With this thought Wassa comforted herself, and watched the school of dolphins rolling about in the foaming water; but all at once they disappeared beneath the surface, and Wassa gave a scream of horror.

Almost before the last echo of the scream had died away, however, they all reappeared in the distance, the fairy prince seated on the dolphin as securely as ever.

"O prince," cried Wassa imploringly, "do not go so far, I pray thee. What will the king say to me if anything should happen to thee? *Do* come back."

"I'll not come back. Ta-ta, ta-ta!
Give my love to my royal pa!"

called out the naughty little prince, waving his hand in adieu to Wassa as the dolphins steered for the open sea.

Wassa, in her distress, ran distractedly up and down, wringing her hands and moaning.

"What will the king say to me? The least he can do will be to chop my head off!" cried poor Wassa. "Oh! what shall I do? Oh! if somebody would only tell me what I am to do!"

"The mid-day moon beneath the sea
Shines in the realms of mermaids free,"

chanted a voice that sounded like a gentle breeze blowing through a grove of pines.

"But I have no idea where the mermaids live, or how to reach the land," answered Wassa sadly.

Again the voice repeated:—

"The mid-day moon beneath the sea
Shines in the realms of mermaids free."

"I never heard of a mid-day moon," said poor Wassa, "but I don't know why there shouldn't be one as well as a midnight sun. I am ready to believe anything now, since I have seen real giants and fairies and mermaids, and if I can find my way to the land of the mid-day moon I'll go there, for anything is better than staying here alone on this desert island."

As Wassa finished speaking, her attention was caught by a large piece of kelp that floated to her feet and stopped. The leaf was broad with curling edges, and it floated on the water like a raft.

> "If here thou dost not wish to stay,
> Accept this from the man in gray,"

chanted the same voice Wassa had heard before.

"Anything is better than staying in this lonely island, and I'll try the seaweed," cried Wassa as she joyfully leaped upon the broad kelp.

No sooner was Wassa seated than the kelp left the island, and glided rapidly out to sea.

"After all," thought Wassa, "the little man in gray was not so bad, although he did send me to Fairyland to take care of that spoiled fairy prince."

CHAPTER XIII.

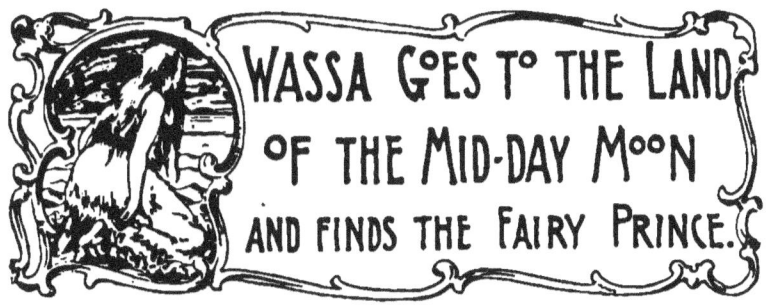

WASSA GOES TO THE LAND OF THE MID-DAY MOON AND FINDS THE FAIRY PRINCE.

The huge kelp glided over the waves so smoothly that Wassa was hardly sensible of any motion. For a time the stillness and the soft sea-breezes were very soothing to her, and she appreciated the rest after the care of her troublesome charge; but gradually Wassa's thoughts reverted to home, and she realized for the first time the anxiety her absence must cause her family.

In imagination the forlorn little maid beheld her brother and sisters roaming through the woods in search of her, and her mother at home anxiously awaiting their return, and then came the thought of her mother's grief when they brought back no news.

"Oh! I must go back," cried Wassa in desperation; "pray take me home again."

No sooner was this wish uttered than the well-known voice answered: —

> "By fairy spells here art thou bound.
> Thy wilful charge must first be found.
> In Fairyland thou needs must stay
> Till set free by the man in gray.
> Be patient, maid, thou shalt find soon
> The land where shines the mid-day moon."

"There is nothing for me to do but to wait until the little man in gray chooses to let me go," thought Wassa desparingly, "but if I have to stay here much longer I will devise some means of escape."

No sooner was this thought formed than the voice answered: —

> "My child, thou'lt learn that no one can
> Succeed without the little gray man."

So Wassa found that it was useless to lay plans for the future, and that the first thing to be done was to find the fairy prince as speedily as possible.

The kelp meanwhile continued its course, and after a time Wassa's eyes fell on a white object that glistened like snow in the distance. As she approached, it took a distinct form, and she beheld a beautiful palace of the purest crystal, that shone with the white light that moonlight alone gives. Soft as the radiance was, it was as light as the most brilliant sunlight.

The kelp glided under the lofty arch that formed the entrance to the temple, and stopped before a flight of white marble steps that stretched downward as far as the eye could reach.

Without hesitation Wassa alighted from the kelp, and it floated away again, and soon passed out of sight. There was but one way to go, and Wassa took it. Down and down she went, the stairs seeming endless, but finally they ceased, and Wassa found herself in a long and lofty hall.

Crystal pillars on each side met overhead and formed shining arches that stretched away in the distance as far as Wassa could see. Columns of beautiful pink and white coral and delicate amber were interspersed with the crystal arches, and over all shone the light of the mid-day moon.

Wassa knew she had now reached the land of the Mid-Day Moon, but where were the mermaidens and where the fairy prince?

> "To reach the spot where mermaids play,
> Sift the gold from the sand away.
> Work with a will, and thou shalt soon
> See the land of the Mid-Day Moon,"

chanted the well-known voice.

Wassa now noticed that the sand under her feet sparkled with grains of gold, but how could she accomplish such an unheard-of task?

"It is of no use to try," thought Wassa, "I can never do it."

THE LAND OF THE MID-DAY MOON. 175

"With patience great, from grains of sand
Was made the great and mighty land.
Shouldst thou refuse, here must thou stay,
So says the little man in gray."

Wassa pondered over these words spoken by the unknown voice. It was evident that the powerful little gray man had made up his mind that she should find the fairy prince, and she had already learned that it was useless to resist the powers in Fairyland; so she at once began to pick out the little specks of gold and lay them in a pile.

The task was a tedious one, but, as the golden pile grew, Wassa's courage grew in proportion, and before long the task was ended.

Then Wassa walked under the lofty arches, until she came to a clear lake, and beyond it the arches still stretched. In the far distance was dimly seen an ocean, whose waters glistened in the beams of the mid-day moon, and shone like emeralds.

"The mermaids must be there," thought Wassa, "but how am I to cross this lake?"

"Dost thou not see the flowers that bloom
In the soft light of the mid-day moon?

> All limp are they for want of rain,
> But thou canst make them fresh again.
> To freshen them, if thou wilt take
> The water of the Crystal Lake,
> Once more will they bloom bright and gay,
> And thou mayst go upon thy way."

Wassa looked about her, and perceived, for the first time, that flowers grew on either side of the path, but the stalks were withered, and the blossoms dingy and shrivelled.

"Am I expected to dip up all the water from that lake?" said Wassa indignantly; "I can never do it."

The unknown voice answered: —

> "Drop by drop, from mist and dew
> Are fed the lakes and ocean blue.
> Here must thou stay till it is done,
> For thou canst not go back alone."

"It is useless for me to resist," said Wassa with a sigh. "It is true I cannot go back alone, so I *must* go on."

As soon as these words were spoken, a cup of gold fell at Wassa's feet, and, picking it up, she filled it at the lake. The instant the rim touched the water, she knew it was a fairy cup, for, small as it was, so much water ran into it that by the time it was full, the waters of the lake had receded perceptibly.

Thus encouraged, Wassa worked diligently, filling her cup and watering the plants. As the first drop touched the leaves, each plant received new life, the withered stalks became once more green and fresh, and the drooping flowers bloomed in gay colors.

So interested did Wassa become in restoring the wilted plants to life, that before she knew it the lake had disappeared, and the path was lined with the gay flowers that bloom only in Fairyland.

Once more Wassa proceeded on her way to the ocean, that appeared to lie as far away as ever, and in the course of her wanderings she came upon a grove of trees laden with the most delicious fruits. Tired and thirsty as she was, this was a tempting sight to Wassa, and she sprang joyfully forward to seize a luscious plum, from which the rich juice was oozing in its ripeness; but as she was about to close her fingers on the tempting fruit, the branches on which it grew sprang out of reach, and a sharp pain in her foot caused her to cry out.

Then Wassa discovered that the ground beneath the trees was covered with brambles, and a sharp thorn from one of them had pierced her foot. At that moment the unknown voice said:—

"My little maid, dost thou not know
'Tis Fairyland where these fruits grow,
And that of them thou canst not eat?
But clear the brambles at thy feet,
And then thy path it will be clear.
The mermaids' home is very near."

"I cannot clear away all these prickly brambles," cried Wassa as she sank down despairingly. "The mermaids are as far away as when I first started, and I shall not go a step farther."

The voice answered:—

"It is but a few steps more,
When thou'lt safely reach the shore
Where the lovely mermaids stay,
With them the fairy prince at play."

"If it is really true that I am so near them as that, I may as well go on, for I can never go back without the prince," said Wassa, and she set to work vigorously at this new task.

The brambles, too, Wassa discovered were fairy brambles, for the instant she made up her mind to undertake the task, not a thorn pricked her, and in a short time the ground was clear.

As Wassa rose to her feet after her labor was over, a fine ripe peach hung before her very mouth, and she could not resist the temptation of reaching out her hand for it. She expected to see the branch spring out of reach, but to her surprise the peach fell into her hand, and she put her lips to the juicy fruit.

Never in her whole life had Wassa tasted anything so delicious, and as she went on her way she gathered many more. When she emerged from the grove, she found herself on the shore of the beautiful green sea she had seen in the distance, and above it stood the full, round mid-day moon. A murmur of rippling water fell on her ears, and riding on the white-capped waves were the mermaids and the fairy prince.

"Prince!" cried Wassa joyfully, "dear prince! At last I have found thee again! Come back at once to the palace. The king will be alarmed at thy long delay."

The prince, however, did not reply, but continued his sport, and Wassa renewed her entreaties.

"*Do* come back," she cried. "If thou couldst know what I have undergone to find thee, I am sure thou wouldst not refuse me."

> "No, no! I will not go, I say;
> With pretty mermaids I will stay.
> Through the green sea I like to glide,
> And on the white-capped waves I ride."

At this reply poor Wassa was in despair. Meanwhile the mermaidens floated on the water, weaving pearls and shining sea-grass in their beautiful hair, and gazing at the charming pictures reflected in their mirrors. They looked so smiling and happy that Wassa found courage to appeal to them.

"O beautiful mermaidens," she cried, extending her hands imploringly, "take pity on me. All this dreary way have I come to find this wilful prince, and hard tasks have I undertaken in order to find him. Now he refuses to go back with me, and how can I face King Rondo without him? Pray take pity on me, beautiful mermaidens, and persuade him to return with me."

The mermaids ceased to adorn their tresses, and gazed at Wassa for the first time. Her face was worn and weary and tear-stained, and the first approach to compassion they had ever felt, came into their cold hearts.

All at once a gentle melody rose on the air, that kept time to the waves rippling against the shore, and as Wassa listened, all sense of her trials left her, and weariness vanished.

As the mermaids sang, the naughty little prince seemed to lose his desire to sport, and floated passively on the waves. Soon his bright eyes grew dreamy, and the lids closed, then opened, then closed again, and as the song ceased they opened no more, and the little fairy prince was in the land of dreams.

Carefully the mermaids placed the sleeping prince in Wassa's arms, and she bore him away. Through the long and lofty arches Wassa carried her sleeping charge, through the fruit grove, and along the path bordered by the gayly blooming flowers, until she reached the long flight of marble steps that led up from the land of the Mid-Day Moon.

Long and tedious had the way down the marble staircase seemed to Wassa, but before she had thought herself to be half way up, she found herself standing in the portal of the crystal palace, and at her feet the fairy kelp. Quickly seating herself in the fairy craft, it put itself in motion, and continued its course until it reached the outlet of the brook.

Then, holding the fairy prince with great care lest he should awake and refuse to be taken home, Wassa stepped ashore, and the fairy kelp glided out to sea.

Wassa had thought to walk the remainder of the way, but there was the fairy boat with the butterfly sails awaiting them, and entering it, it sailed rapidly up the stream until it reached the spot where it had first appeared. Wassa stepped ashore once more, and the fairy boat glided down the stream and was soon out of sight.

Then, carrying her still sleeping charge in her arms, Wassa reached the palace, and laid him in his bed. A minute more and Wassa's hard experiences of the day were forgotten in a sound and dreamless sleep.

CHAPTER XIV.

THE FAIRY PRINCE AND WASSA.

The next morning Wassa was awakened by the voice of the little prince calling to her:—

> "Wake up, wake up, my nurse, I say!
> The prairies wild I'll see to-day!
> In the tall grass I'll lie and hide,
> And buffaloes I mean to ride."

"No, no, prince, lie down and have another nap first," said Wassa, who felt she had not had half sleep enough; but the persistent prince was not to be put off so easily, and clamored loudly to be taken at once to the prairies.

"The prairies are so far away," argued Wassa, "and I am so very tired. I will take thee to the grotto where the gold fishes are, and thou canst play with them."

At this proposition the naughty little prince stamped his feet and screamed loudly:—

> "No, thou bad nurse, I tell thee no!
> I do not wish with thee to go.

> The prairie lands are not too far;
> Go, or I'll scream and wake my pa!"

Poor Wassa was in despair. Another such day as that she had passed in Fairyland, she felt would be unendurable, but what could she do? There stood the wayward prince, stamping and screaming and, like many another child not of royal blood, keeping his eyes on his victim to see if she showed any signs of relenting.

"I will not give in to this spoiled child," thought Wassa; "if I do, there will be no end to his freaks, and he may take it into his head to go up to the moon."

The shrewd fairy prince fathomed the depths of Wassa's mind, and he set up such a resounding cry, that in a few moments King Rondo appeared, looking as if he had been suddenly awakened from a sound sleep, and such in fact was the case.

> "Hey dey! hey day! what's all this din?"
> Said Rondo, as he strode within.
> "What is it now? I pray thee tell
> The meaning of that fearful yell
> That made my skin like goose-flesh creep,
> And roused me from my morning sleep."

"Sire," answered Wassa humbly, "I am very sorry, but I was trying to persuade the prince to give up his project of going to the prairies to-day."

Here the prince broke in vociferously: —

> "To prairies I will go to-day!
> Pa, make her go with me, I say."

Wassa's heart sank within her as the king replied: —

> "Thy will is law, and shall be done;
> Truly thou shalt go, my son.
> And now to sleep once more I'll try.
> Don't let me hear another cry."

As the king left the apartment, poor Wassa sank back with her face hidden in her hands, and gave way to tears of disappointment and vexation. For a moment the prince looked at her with the comical expression that the elf Toto was wont to wear, then cried in the voice of the wayward prince: —

> "Wassa, thou wilt have to go, —
> My pa has said it shall be so.
> If not, I'll scream, — my pa will come,
> And then thou'lt see what will be done."

"I know what *ought* to be done, and what would be if I were thy pa," exclaimed Wassa, beside herself with vexation.

Another comical look of the elf Toto twinkled for an instant in the fairy prince's eye, but it vanished before Wassa caught it, and the imperious prince opened his mouth to utter another loud cry, when Wassa quickly caught him up in her arms, saying: —

"Oh! do hush, and I'll take thee to the world's end, thou naughty child."

So off set the prince and Wassa on their expedition to the prairies.

For a time the road lay through broad fields covered with velvety grass and bright flowers, and along gently running brooks; but gradually the scene changed. Instead of the smooth fields, forests appeared, and the brooks no longer flowed peacefully, but rushed tumultuously onward, foaming and gurgling as they went.

Wassa, carrying her charge, soon grew weary, after she had left the smooth fields, and her tired feet stumbled over the rough stones and uneven ground.

"I cannot go to the prairies!" exclaimed

Wassa as she bruised her foot against a jagged stone that lay in the path. "I will remain here, and thou canst play in this foaming brook."

But the wilful prince cried: —

> "No, no, I say, I'll not stay here;
> I wish to see the pretty deer."

"I shall not take thee to see them," replied Wassa decidedly. "I am too tired to carry thee any farther," and she sank down by the brook side.

Seeing this, the prince, gazing toward the forest that lay about them as far as the eye could reach, said: —

> "Thou pretty deer so strong and fleet,
> Bear us on with nimble feet.
> Through these forests deep now hie,
> Seek the land where prairies lie."

No sooner were these words spoken than a rustling of the forest branches was heard, and a beautiful deer with head erect and branching horns sprang from out the forest, and, bounding toward the fairy prince and Wassa, dropped gracefully on his knees before them, and bowed his delicate head in token of submission.

Without a word the prince and Wassa seated themselves on the beautiful creature's back, and he bounded away into the depths of the forest.

As swift as the wind moves, the fairy deer bounded over foaming brooks and rocks, and through the tall underbrush of the forest, that parted on either side as he sped onward.

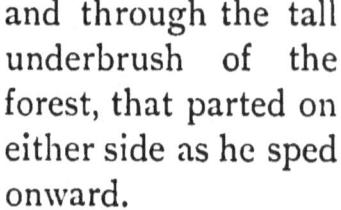

By degrees the wood became more dense, the trees grew more lofty, and the brooks became broader and rushed more wildly along, forming cascades and waterfalls that murmured loudly in the silent forest. The path, too, grew rocky and steep, but the fairy deer flew up the steep ascents as lightly as he had skimmed over the level ground of the forest.

At last the deer came to a standstill before

a range of mountains that rose in lofty peaks before the travellers, and a broad river flowed at their feet. Gently the deer once more knelt, and his riders dismounted. The instant they were on the ground the deer bounded away again, and was lost to view in the thick forest.

"Now," said Wassa as she looked at the broad river before her and the range of lofty mountains beyond, "what will happen next? Shall we go by the river, or shall we climb over those high mountains?"

The fairy prince made no reply, but seemed intent on watching a large eagle that was circling over one of the highest mountain peaks. So great was the height that he looked like a little black speck against the sky. The prince, keeping his eye on the bird, recited these lines:—

"Come hither, I pray, king of the sky,
Bear us over these mountains high."

The black speck grew larger and larger as the bird seemed to drop down from his great height, and soon the form of an immense eagle was distinctly visible.

The huge bird descended in graceful circles,

and at last alighted at the feet of the fairy prince.

The large, strong wings, the fierce bent beak, and the piercing eyes of the eagle filled Wassa with awe, but the fairy prince jumped lightly and confidently upon his back, and Wassa took her place beside him. The eagle spread his long wings and soared into the sky

Higher and higher flew the eagle, but so steadily that no motion was perceptible, and soon the forest and river below could hardly be discerned.

Over the tall mountains flew the eagle, and the snow-clad peaks shone white and cold beneath them. Occasionally their swift flight started a bear from its hidden retreat, and he slunk away growling defiance. Large snakes, too, lying on sunny slopes trying to catch the warming rays of the sun, wriggled into their holes as their dreaded enemy, the eagle, flew above them.

After a time the eagle began to descend, and flying nearer the forests and rivers, finally alighted.

The fairy prince and Wassa dismounted, and the eagle, swiftly soaring once more high into the sky, disappeared from their view.

Wassa gazed about her. She knew they must have reached the prairies, for level land stretched away in every direction. Tall, waving grass grew at their feet, and not a living creature was in sight to break the silence.

"How forlorn!" cried Wassa with a shudder. "Why didst thou wish to come here? Do go directly, for there is nothing here for thee to play with."

> "In the tall grass I'll play and hide,
> And buffaloes I mean to ride,"

replied the prince.

"But there are no buffaloes here," said

Wassa, "and it is fortunate for us that there are not. Pray call the eagle to take us back."

> "O buffalo so wild and free!
> I pray thee come and play with me.
> We'll roam across the prairies wide,
> And in the waving grasses hide."

No sooner were these words spoken by the fairy prince than the trampling of feet was heard, and a herd of buffaloes was seen rushing toward the prince and Wassa.

Wassa shuddered with fear as the great creatures with their huge heads and strong horns rushed madly onward and stopped before the prince. They tossed their heads with their thick manes, and snorted wildly, pawing the ground with their strong hoofs.

The prince, however, evinced no fear of the fierce creatures, and stroked their great heads, which they bent down, while they rubbed their noses affectionately against him.

The largest and fiercest of the buffaloes, the leader of the herd, kept by the prince's side, pushing aside the heads of the others, that he alone might receive the caresses of the little prince. The remainder of the herd closed around the prince, until he was hidden from Wassa's sight, and she became alarmed lest their great feet should trample him to death.

"Prince!" cried Wassa, "do come away from those great beasts; they will surely trample thee to death."

Great were Wassa's surprise and terror, as the herd parted for an instant, to see the little prince seated on the back of the leader, holding one horn lightly with his little hand, and his face full of merriment.

"Come back!" cried Wassa, springing toward the herd, as they began to move off in the direction whence they had appeared; "thou wilt be lost. Do not trust to those wild creatures. Oh! what will the king say?"

But the prince rejoined, laughing merrily: —

> "They are not wild; with them I'll go.
> Thou know'st my royal pa said so."

As the prince ceased, the buffaloes tossed their heads, pawing the earth as they snorted loudly; then, with lowered heads, they set off across the prairie with the speed of the wind. The prince waved his hand joyously as he was borne away, and Wassa was left alone on the wide prairie.

"What shall I do? What shall I do?" moaned Wassa, wringing her hands in despair. "I cannot go back, or I shall die in this horrible desert. Oh! if I only knew where the prince has gone!"

A voice was heard to say: —

> "The wilful prince has gone to play
> In the land of the Starlit Day."

"But I never heard of the land of the Starlit Day," cried Wassa. "How can I find it?"

> "Through the prairie the way is found.
> Go, till thou reach a tiny mound.
> Sentries three on duty stay,
> To guard the land of the Starlit Day."

Thus chanted the voice Wassa had heard before.

"I shall have to go on, I suppose," said Wassa, "for I shall die of fright here in this wilderness."

So saying, Wassa started in search of the land of the Starlit Day.

The tall prairie grass grew all about her, and she pushed her way resolutely through it. On and on she went until her feet were weary, and an intense hunger took possession of her, for she had eaten nothing but fruit since her sojourn in Fairyland.

Endless seemed the tall prairie grass, and not a sign of the three sentinels appeared.

"I don't believe there is any such land at all, and I may as well die here as anywhere," said poor Wassa, throwing herself down upon the soft dry grass.

> "Patience, patience; soon thou'lt be
> Where on guard are sentries three,"

was heard from the unknown voice; and Wassa took courage and went boldly on.

Soon the little maid's efforts were rewarded by finding the tall prairie grass growing thinner and shorter, and she could now look about her. In the distance she beheld a mound, on the top of which she descried two small objects, but what they were she could not discover. Hastening her steps, Wassa hurried toward this welcome sight, and, before long discovered that the two objects that had attracted her attention were a little prairie-dog and an owl.

"This must be the place," said Wassa to

herself. "Here is the mound, and here are two of the sentries, but where is the third?"

As she spoke, a third object appeared at the opening in the mound, and Wassa started nervously as the dark head of a rattlesnake came into view. It reared itself cautiously from the opening, as if it did not like to attract attention, and looked cautiously at the little maid.

Cautious, however, as were the rattlesnake's movements, they attracted the attention of the watchful owl, whose great yellow eyes were instantly fixed upon it.

"Go back at once and attend to thy cooking," said the owl severely. "Don't let the rabbit-stew be burnt again to-day."

The snake jerked back her head with great alacrity, and disappeared within the hole, and Wassa now perceived a fragrant odor of cooking viands proceeding from within the mound.

Meanwhile the owl and the prairie-dog were regarding the little maid with great curiosity.

CHAPTER XV.

WASSA CAPTURES THE FAIRY PRINCE.

Wassa was certain that the opening in the mound led to the land of the Starlit Day, but she hesitated before she could make up her mind to enter the dark passageway that led to the underground realms.

The little prairie-dog was certainly not to be feared, and the owl, although so dignified and majestic in her bearing, was also harmless; but when the little maid thought of meeting the rattlesnake in the dark, her courage sank, and she stood irresolute, gazing into the darkness that extended as far as she could see.

> "Fear not, maiden; yon's the way
> Leading to the starlit day:
> Boldly enter, have no fear;
> Whom thou seekest, he is near."

These words, spoken by the well-known voice, gave Wassa courage, and she boldly entered the dark hole. At first she could see nothing, but as soon as her eyes became accustomed to the change, she was surprised to find that she could see as well as if it were daylight.

The passageway was narrow at first, and so low that Wassa was obliged to crawl on her hands and knees. As she proceeded, the odor of savory food that she had perceived as she stood outside, grew still more pleasant, and the hunger that had been gradually increasing, grew almost unbearable.

By degrees the passage widened, and she found before long that she could stand erect, so she rose to her feet and walked rapidly forward. A dim light in the distance, and a slender, dark object that constantly moved to and fro in front of it, attracted the little maid's attention, and soon she came into a large cavern, and discovered that the light came from a fire, over which a kettle was hanging, from which clouds of fragrant vapor issued. The slender, dark object was the rattlesnake she had seen before, and so dreaded to meet.

Wassa's fears, however, were unfounded, for the rattlesnake, in her capacity of cook, was far too anxious in the cooking of the rabbit-stew to pay any heed to strangers. Restlessly moving to and fro, she constantly reared her head to gaze into the kettle, to see if the stew were in danger of burning.

"Oh, deary me! deary me! if it should catch on again to-day!" murmured the poor cook, in a helpless, dazed sort of way.

One of the peculiarities of Fairyland is, that those who enter there can understand the animal language, and Wassa was surprised to find how easily she understood the rattlesnake. The fear she had first felt now vanished as she watched the feeble-minded cook, and her hunger increased as the savory odors of the stew grew more and more fragrant.

"Oh, deary me! if it should catch on again to-day!" again murmured the poor cook, after another peep into the kettle. "And I wonder if I have forgotten to put the salt in to-day. Can any one tell me if I have forgotten to put the salt in to-day?"

"Yes, madam," said Wassa politely, advancing toward the distracted cook, " I can tell thee, if thou wilt let me have a taste;" and Wassa's mouth fairly watered at the thought of the savory dish.

" What is that to thee, pray?" said the cook in an irritable tone. " I forgot the salt yesterday, and she was very angry, and if I forget it again to-day, I don't know what she will do to me. Oh! will any one tell me if I have forgotten to put it in to-day?"

" How can any one tell thee unless thou art willing to let them taste of it?" said Wassa, out of patience with the foolish cook.

"What has that to do with it?" asked the snake, shaking her rattles severely. "I forgot it yesterday, and she told me not to forget it again. Oh! if somebody would only tell me if I have forgotten it to-day!"

"That's the strangest way of reasoning *I* ever heard of," said Wassa to herself. " But if she will not listen to me, I can't help her. I wish I could get some of that stew, salt or no salt, it smells so good."

The rattlesnake still watched anxiously the rabbit-stew, breaking out at intervals into the same expressions regarding the burning on and the salt, and her fear of the owl's dipleasure. At last Wassa could bear it no longer, and exclaimed : —

"Do let me have a little of the stew, it smells so deliciously, and I am almost starved."

As Wassa spoke, she picked up a dish that lay on the ground, and boldly approached the kettle.

"Stop!" cried the rattlesnake, "thou must not do that! Nobody but she must touch it, and even the other one does not dare to so much as look at it until she has had all she wants. And as for me, why, if I get the kettle to lap out, it's as much as ever I get. Then dost thou suppose I would let thee have any?"

Wassa was too hungry to be easily put aside, and with a determined air attempted to dip up some of the stew, but the snake sprang her rattle loudly, at the same time rearing her head upright and preparing to spring; but at the sight of the rattlesnake's flattened head and vicious expression, Wassa quickly threw down the dish and darted away. When at a safe distance, she looked back, and saw the rattlesnake once more engrossed in her cooking, and muttering distractedly to herself as before.

The passageway into which Wassa had turned grew narrow, and she was obliged once more to creep on her hands and knees. In this way she proceeded for some time, until her back became so stiff and her arms and knees so lame that she could hardly move, and she thought she could go no farther, but in the distance, all at once, appeared a beautiful rosy light. Her courage revived, and she hastened to reach it.

Before long the passage grew higher and broader, and she again rose to her feet, and hurried toward the light. Suddenly the passage opened into a lofty cavern, the shining walls of which were of pure rock-salt, and a bright, rosy light fell over all, causing the crystals to shine until her eyes could hardly bear the brilliancy.

"Oh, how beautiful!" exclaimed Wassa as she gazed about her in wonder.

At that moment the gurgling of a waterfall fell on her ears, and she beheld a beautiful fountain sending streams of rosy-tinted water high into the air.

"Now I can quench my thirst," cried Wassa

as she sprang joyfully toward the fountain; but as she stooped to put her lips to the cool water, in the distance she caught a glimpse of the fairy prince, whom she was so eager to find.

"Prince! Prince!" cried Wassa loudly, running toward him, "stop, pray stop!" but the prince did not heed her call, and ran on faster than before.

The poor little maid cast one look of regret at the tempting fountain, and then continued her pursuit of the fairy prince. The passage again grew narrow, and she was once more obliged to creep her way along; and the fairy prince was now out of sight. But Wassa knew that her only safety was in going forward, and she continued her way, until, weary and faint from hunger and thirst, she at last descried in the distance a pale blue light. Making her way toward the welcome sight, the passage grew wider, and soon led into a large blue grotto, lined with silver ore.

If the first grotto, with its rosy-tinted lights falling on the sparkling walls of salt, had appeared beautiful, how much more beautiful did this shining silver grotto appear, with the soft blue light pervading it!

Tired and faint as Wassa was, in a moment she forgot her weariness and faintness as she gazed rapturously on the beauties about her; but before her eyes had feasted themselves on these wonders, a slight sound arrested her attention, and there was the fairy prince just before her, and roguishly laughing back at her as he ran.

"I will catch thee this time," cried Wassa, springing toward him, "if I die in the attempt;" and away through a narrow archway that led from the grotto fled the fairy prince, with Wassa close at his heels.

On and on through crooked descents went the two, and many a time Wassa's hand nearly grasped the little prince, but each time he bounded lightly away, and at last disappeared altogether from her sight.

More determined than ever to overtake her wayward charge, Wassa made a desperate attempt, and struggled on, weary and faint from hunger and thirst, until her tired limbs refused to obey her will, and she sank exhausted on the ground.

> "Courage, maid, an effort make,
> And the prince thou'lt overtake.

206   THE FAIRY-FOLK OF THE BLUE HILL.

Reach yon bright and shining light,
And all thy wrongs shall be set right."

As Wassa heard these words, she opened

her heavy eyes, and saw a brilliant light in front of her, and gathering new hope from the promise of the voice, she pushed wearily on. In a few moments she stood in a lofty grotto, the sides of which seemed to be of burnished gold, and a brilliant light, clear and soft as starlight, but a thousand times brighter, shone over all.

As Wassa looked admiringly about her, a light form stood before her, robed in gauzy dress that shone like the stars, and above her head glistened a large star that scintillated as she moved. With a kindly smile the beautiful being spoke: —

> "Rough the path, and long the way
> Leading to the starlit day.
> Eat this fruit, and thou shalt see
> Hunger will appeasèd be."

As the fairy spoke, she held a large and juicy plum toward Wassa, who seized it eagerly. No sooner had it touched her lips than all sense of hunger and thirst vanished, and she felt as much refreshed as if she had partaken of a hearty repast.

The fairy, regarding Wassa with the same kindly smile, continued: —

> "Maiden, thou canst not thyself
> Catch that sprightly, roguish elf.
> Since thy duty is done well,

Thou shalt have a fairy spell.
Soon the prince will come this way,
To him thou these words must say: —

>Toto the Slim,
>   I know thee well,
> And o'er thee cast
>   This fairy spell.
> I have thee now, —
>   No more thou'lt roam,
> But seek at once
>   Thy fairy home.

While thou chantest, o'er him shower
Petals of this fairy flower.
Perfumes sweet that in it dwell
Work o'er him a fairy spell."

As the fairy ceased, she held a bright flower toward Wassa, the perfume of which was so sweet that it pervaded the whole grotto in an instant. Before the little maid had time to thank her, the fairy had vanished. At the same moment Wassa espied the little prince, and, bounding toward him, she shook the flower over him, at the same time saying: —

> "Toto the Slim,
>   I know thee well,
> And o'er thee cast
>   This fairy spell.

> I have thee now, —
>   No more thou'lt roam,
>   But seek at once
>   Thy fairy home."

The instant the fairy flower was shaken o'er him, the fairy prince stood as if spellbound, and Wassa easily picked him up and set off for home.

Through other long and dreary passages Wassa carried her charge, who from time to time struggled to free himself from her tight grasp, but every time she shook the fairy flower over him he ceased to struggle, and they proceeded for a while quietly on their way.

Wassa's long journey, however, had told heavily upon her, and the prince's struggles to free himself as often as the fairy flower lost its influence, tired and irritated her. Many a time she was on the point of abandoning her project of reaching King Rondo's domains, but as often as she gave way to this impulse came the thought of the dreadful fate that would be hers if she should have to stay in these underground caverns, — for no sound, either of man or beast, reached her, — and so she continued her dreary way until a huge rock that towered upward like a mountain rose before her and barred her way.

What was to be done? To go back the same way was impossible, and Wassa sank on the ground in despair; but even in her desperation she kept fast hold of the fairy prince. All at once she heard the prince speak these words: —

"Rockroller, come to me, I pray,
And roll this mighty stone away."

At these words, Wassa looked up, and saw, over the top of the huge rock, the head of a giant, whose sleepy, good-natured face looked as if he had been aroused from a sound nap. In a moment the giant stood before them, yawning and stretching to awaken himself. Easily lifting the huge rock with one hand, he tossed it lightly aside, and, to Wassa's astonishment, the domains of King Rondo lay before her.

In her surprise, Wassa had dropped, without

knowing it, the fairy flower that had wrought such a wondrous change in the prince's mood; but no sooner was the flower gone than the prince renewed his struggles with greater energy than before, screaming and kicking so that Wassa could scarcely hold him.

> "I won't go back with thee, I say!
> I like the land of the Starlit Day.
> If thou dost not obey me quick,
> Then I will loudly scream and kick."

At these words of the fairy prince, Wassa's stock of patience was wholly exhausted, and she exclaimed:—

"Kick and scream as loudly as thou canst; I am stronger than thou art, and thou shalt not escape me again;" and, despite the screaming and struggling of the naughty prince, she held him firmly in her arms, and did not release him until she found King Rondo, when she placed his son before him, saying angrily:—

"I have brought the prince back safely this time, but not all the treasures of thy kingdom would tempt me to take care of him another day; for of all the spoiled children I ever saw, he is the worst, and, after seeing him, I wonder that I could ever have thought dear little Mona a spoiled child, just because she had pretty things and liked to wear them."

The king, as Wassa began to speak, had regarded her with knitted brows, but gradually his face relaxed, and, as she finished, the good-natured twinkle of the eye that characterized his expression, once more appeared, and he spoke thus: —

"Little maid, although we fairy folk are unknown to thee, thou hast long been known by us, and we have watched over thee. The envy of thy friend Mona that was in thy heart troubled us sorely, and all the naughty tricks thou hast put upon her were known to us. We resolved to cure thee of this fault, and to show thee what a spoiled child really was. For this reason we made a spoiled child of Toto the Slim, and well must he have played his part, since thou confessest that thou wast mistaken in thy judgment of Mona. Now, since thou hast discovered thy fault, thou canst depart from Fairyland, but thou know'st the consequences if thou repeatest thy fault."

Whereupon King Rondo signalled to his gnomes, saying: —

"Ho, vassals! Ope the portal wide,
That this fair maid may pass outside."

Then the huge wall of rock rolled aside, and as Wassa passed through, a voice said: —

"Broken the spell, the task is done,
A battle hard thou here hast won.
Envious thoughts keep from thy door,
So dwell in peace for evermore."

As the words ceased, the door rolled back into place, and Wassa found herself standing alone on the top of Blue Hill. The sun had disappeared behind the western woods, and its last rosy tints were reflected from its summit. Wassa walked rapidly down through the land of the After-glow. All was still; the only living creature in sight was the blue dragon-fly, who was returning from a gay party among the lily-pads of the pond.

CHAPTER XVI.

CLOUDCATCHER AND HIS PRISONERS.

When King Rondo ordered the door to be opened for Wassa to leave his domains, there was an observer who carefully noted everything that took place. This was no other than the giant king, Cloudcatcher. Seated on the summit of a neighboring spur of Blue Hill, he saw what went on for miles about,— saw the elf Toto, whom he supposed to be the fairy prince, and watched Wassa as she walked through the door.

The reason for King Cloudcatcher's watching the entrance to the gnomes' cavern was this: when the giant Rockroller removed the rock for Wassa and her charge to leave the land of the Starlit Day, he did not recognize the elf Toto the Slim in his disguise of the fairy prince, and, thinking him to be really the son of King Rondo, he acquainted King Cloudcatcher with the fact, and the giant king at once conceived the idea of capturing the young

CLOUDCATCHER AND HIS PRISONERS. 215

prince and holding him, thus paying back the many tricks the gnomes had played upon the giants.

So great was King Cloudcatcher's excitement at the prospect of an opportunity to ob-

tain possession of the young prince, that he did not look as carefully as he should have done, or he would have discovered that Wassa left the gnomes' kingdom alone.

Stepping over the tall trees that lay in his path, and trying to make as little noise as possible, King Cloudcatcher, holding his hood in his hand, after the manner of a boy who is trying to catch a butterfly, came up behind Wassa at the very moment when she met the blue dragon-fly, and, being as we said before, nervous and hasty, and, moreover, never noted for the sharpness of his wits, he hastily threw his hood over Wassa and the blue dragon-fly, and, tucking it under his arm, strode rapidly off with his prize, never doubting for a moment that he had captured the fairy prince and his nurse.

A few long steps brought King Cloudcatcher to the ocean, and he skirted along the edges to cool his feet to prepare them for his long walk. Then he stepped across to the Isles of Shoals, as they are now called, and sat for a moment's rest on the island of Appledore.

All this time the giant held his hood securely under his arm, but dared not take a good look at his prisoners for fear the wilful prince might take advantage of the opportunity to escape.

When sufficiently cooled off, King Cloudcatcher resumed his journey, wading across to New Hampshire in a few good strides, and then heading straight for the White Mountains.

The cries from within the hood reached him only as confused murmurs, and the giant's head was so high among the clouds that he did not hear accurately what went on so far below him. He walked through Lake Winnipesaukee to wash the dust from his feet, and in a few minutes stood at the foot of Mt. Washington.

By this time the cries from Wassa and the blue dragon-fly had grown very faint, for between terror and fatigue they were too much exhausted to make much noise. A few vigorous strides took the giant to the summit of the mountain, and, stopping before a cave made for the purpose by the giant Rockroller, King Cloudcatcher thrust in his captives and hastily barred the entrance with a large rock.

When the cavern was closed, the giant king, elated with the success of his plan, indulged in a fit of hearty laughter that echoed like a volley of artillery among the mountain ranges, and struck terror to the hearts of the two poor little prisoners within the cave.

The king's return trip was made in a much shorter time than the one we have just described, and he quickly summoned his subjects to a conference. When they were all assembled, the king addressed them in his usual pompous manner:—

"While ye have been idling away your time, ye dull knaves, your king has been busy. If he had not more brains than the whole of ye put together, the dwarf prince would never have been captured. As it is, he is at this moment safe in our cavern on yonder mountain."

"Is that true, your majesty?" ejaculated the giants in a breath.

"Indeed, it is the very truth," replied King Cloudcatcher.

"How did it happen?" asked one of the giants humbly.

"There is no need to acquaint thee with the tale," replied the king. "It suffices that the thing is done. The only consideration now is, how to obtain an interview with the dwarf king and force him to compromise. Now that his son and heir is in our hands we can make our own terms. The question then is, how can we gain access to him?"

As the giant king ceased, Toto the Slim stood before him, and, bowing low, said:—

> "Most gracious king, I have the right
> The gnome to seek, by day or night.

So, mighty king, I prithee say
If I can aid in any way."

The giant king looked down upon the tiny elf that hardly reached to his ankle, but who stood before the tall giant with as independent an air as if he were as tall as the tallest of them.

"Yes, friend elf," answered King Cloudcatcher, "thou canst do me a great service. Thou know'st well the feud that exists between us and the dwarfs. We have captured the dwarf prince and have him safely imprisoned in yonder distant mountain. There shall he stay until the dwarf king agrees to resign his crown and acknowledge us as the rightful king. Wilt thou undertake the commission?"

"Thou hast done well to imprison the dwarf prince," replied the elf, "for I know him to be wilful and peevish. It will do him good to stay in prison for a time. I will repair to the gnome king and inform him that his son and heir is in thy power and there will remain until he agrees to thy conditions, which are, to give up everything and acknowledge thee as his lawful king. Have I learned my task rightly?"

"Thou art a knowing elf," answered King Cloudcatcher, "and hast learned thy task well. Go at once to the dwarf king, and lay the case before him. We will await his answer here, and rest after our trip to yonder hill."

So saying, the giant threw himself down in an easy position, and in a moment his heavy breathing swayed the tall forest trees about and whistled through their sturdy branches.

Toto the Slim watched the sleeping giant for a moment with great enjoyment, then bounded up the hill, and in a twinkling stood before the high rock that shut in King Rondo's domains. The signal was given, the rock rolled back, and Toto entered the cavern. Proceeding at once to the king's banquet hall, he found his majesty seated before his favorite dish of "grubs on toast."

"Why com'st thou in such haste?" asked the gnome king as he finished his last mouthful and, pushing back his chair, looked benignly upon the elf.

"King Rondo," began Toto, "the giant king, Cloudcatcher, bade me acquaint thee with the news that he has thy son and heir in his power, and that there he will remain until thou dost agree to his conditions."

"What may those be, little elf?" asked the king. "Much would I sacrifice to see once more that sweet child, that mild-mannered prince. Methinks I hear even now his dulcet tones. Sleepless at night, not tempted even by the most savory dishes by day" (here a merry twinkle came into the king's bright eyes as he glanced at the empty dish), "I shall know no peaceful moments until I behold the fairy prince once more. Tell me, then, the conditions, friend elf."

"The conditions, my liege, are these: that thou dost resign all right to thy kingdom and acknowledge Cloudcatcher as lawful king."

"And is that all the giant wants?" asked King Rondo. "Say to him that all this and more would I gladly do to receive from him my son and heir. Dost thou remember the sweet prince, friend elf?"

Whereupon the elf began at once to throw his arms about and stamp his feet, crying peevishly:—

"Thou horrid nurse, now go away!
I will not go with thee, I say!"

The king and Toto both laughed immoderately at the recollection of the trick they had played so successfully, and then Toto the Slim bade the king adieu and returned to the giant.

Meantime the giant king was fast asleep at the foot of the hill, but before he had slept many minutes, the elf Toto returned, and, finding the giant asleep still, perched astride the branch of a tall pine that grew above the head of the sleeping giant, and watched him with much amusement.

For a while it was very entertaining to see the giant with his great mouth open, and watch his deep breathing and the stupid expression of his face, but before long the pastime became monotonous, and the elf began to wish he would wake up. As the giant's sleep became heavier and heavier, and the sounds of his breathing louder and louder, the elf grew impatient, and set his active mind at work to discover some means of awakening the great fellow.

Picking up a large stone, or rather one that was large for the elf's small hands, — in fact it was about the size of a large walnut,— the elf climbed the tree once more, holding his stone carefully, and when just above the giant's head he let the stone fall on the sleeping, upturned face. It hit the giant's nose, but it made no more impression on him than a grain of sand would have made upon the elf, in truth, not half so much, and the giant slept more deeply than before.

Finding his first experiment a failure, the elf bethought himself of another. Hastily sliding down the tree, he cast his eyes about until they lighted on a stick pointed at one end.

In reality the stick was a short one, but compared with the height and strength of the elf, it seemed a mighty pole. Firmly seizing the thickest end in both his hands, and holding the pointed end straight before him, as one would handle a spear, the elf started on a run in the direction of the giant's face.

By the time Toto reached the giant he had accumulated a good deal of force, and the sharp point of the stick brought up against the giant's cheek with force sufficient to cause him to put up his hand and make a motion as though he were brushing a mosquito away.

This motion satisfied Toto that he had made some impression upon the thick skin of the giant, and he repeated the thrust several times.

At each prick of the stick the giant rubbed his cheek, but at last his heavy breathing ceased, and he sat upright, exclaiming:—

"The mosquitoes are thick in these low lands. I must choose a loftier site for my nap."

The next moment the giant caught sight of the elf, and at once remembered that he was awaiting him when he fell asleep.

"Well, friend elf," said the giant, "what success hadst thou with the dwarf?"

CHAPTER XVII.

THE LITTLE GRAY MAN'S DECISION.

The elf looked very tiny as he stood before the giant king, who still reclined on the grass, resting his head on his hand; and even in this position the elf was obliged to look upward to see the giant's face.

"Come a little nearer, friend elf," said the giant good-naturedly as he reached out one of his fingers. Toto immediately jumped astride the great finger, and was thus brought on a level with the giant's face.

"Come, my little man, let us now hear the result of thy visit to the dwarf king. What said he?"

With a very serious expression on his rosy little face, the elf replied: —

> "Rondo, great king, is nearly wild
> With grief at loss of his fair child;
> No sleep by night, no food by day
> Since the dear child was stolen away.
> To all thy terms he will agree
> His cherished son and heir to see.

He prays thee no more time to waste,
But bring him back in greatest haste."

"So!" exclaimed King Cloudcatcher with a laugh so loud that it nearly blew the elf from his finger, "I thought we had found the way to his heart. Come, friend elf, since thou hast executed thy mission so well, thou shalt take a journey to yonder high mountain and see the prison where we have the dwarf prince in safe keeping."

So saying, the giant picked up his great hood that lay on the ground beside him, and that was much larger than the hut of either the hunter or the rover, or, in fact, than both put together, and, placing the elf on the top of it, where he could sit or walk about as he felt inclined, and whence he would have a fine view of the country through which they must pass, the giant carefully put his hood on his head, and, rising to his feet, set off once more northward.

This was the first journey the elf had ever taken, and, after he became accustomed to his lofty position, he took great pleasure in looking down upon the landscape that lay so far below him. The effect was much the same, I presume, as travellers in balloons experience. There was one drawback, however, and that was that so high among the clouds the air was very chilly, and Toto's small nose soon became as red as a cherry. The broad surface of the edge of the hood, however, was as good as a race-course, and Toto ran and danced about upon it until his blood was all in a glow.

"Take care, my little man, don't get *too* lively up there and tumble off," the giant king would say from below, when Toto became particularly active; and the mischief-loving and nimble elf would reply by redoubling his efforts, turning summersaults, and sometimes dropping over the edge of the hood, as if he were about to fall, and then, by a nimble movement, recovering himself and springing back again.

These feints of Toto made the giant quite

nervous, and it is needless to say gave the mischievous elf great satisfaction.

In this manner the two proceeded until they reached the top of Mt. Washington, when the giant paused before the cave in which his two prisoners were confined. They, hearing the giant's approach, set up a clamor to be released, and at the sound of the voices the giant smiled with great satisfaction.

"Now, my little man," said the giant, taking off his hood and carefully picking Toto up between his forefinger and thumb, "we will put thee in a place of safety, whence thou canst see what passes. The dwarf prince is so small and full of tricks that he may escape us, if we are not on our guard."

So saying, King Cloudcatcher placed Toto the Slim upon a fir tree that grew near by, and began to move away cautiously the great stone that stood before the mouth of the cave.

When a small opening was effected, Cloudcatcher bent over and looked into the cave. It was very dark within, but he could discern the rover's little maid standing ready to come out as soon as the stone was removed. While the giant was looking eagerly for the fairy prince, something fluttered by him and flew quickly away. It was the blue dragon-fly, who, delighted at being released, betook herself home as fast as her wings could carry her.

"Oh! it's thou, my little lady, is it?" exclaimed the giant as his eyes followed the dragon-fly, who was fast disappearing in the distance. "Well, our business is not with thee."

The stone was removed, and out walked Wassa.

"Where is the prince, my maid?" asked the giant anxiously as his eyes peered into the dark cave. "What hast thou done with thy charge, the dwarf prince?"

"The fairy prince dost thou mean?" asked Wassa, surprised. "What have *I* done with him? Why, I am but too thankful to *be* done with him. Where should he be but in the realms of King Rondo, his father?"

"Stay!" thundered the giant as Wassa was about to depart; "do not trifle with me, or thou shalt learn what it is to offend the giant king. I ask thee once again, where is the dwarf prince, whom I imprisoned with thee in this cave? Answer me truly, for if I find thou art deceiving me, thou shalt pay dearly for it."

"Sire," answered Wassa humbly, and trembling before the loud tones of the angry giant, "I have not deceived thee. On my way down the hill, after King Rondo set me free from Fairyland, I was suddenly caught up and brought to this place. Not a living creature was with me, except a blue dragon-fly, who was passing at the time. She has just flown away, and I pray thee to allow me to depart too."

"The prince! the dwarf prince!" thundered the enraged giant, who began to believe that he had been duped. "I ask thee for the last time, where is the dwarf prince?"

As soon as the blue dragon-fly had made her escape, the elf Toto the Slim, unperceived by the giant or Wassa, had slid down from the fir tree, and crept up behind the giant, and before poor frightened Wassa could reply, the mischievous elf, imitating the fairy prince who had caused Wassa so much trouble, danced up and down, and screamed:—

"No, no! I won't go home, I say!
I'll scream until thou lett'st me stay."

"There he is! There is the fairy prince," cried Wassa as she recognized her former wilful charge.

With an exclamation of joy, Cloudcatcher scooped up the mischievous elf and Wassa, thrust them hurriedly into his hood, and started with his longest strides for home.

Wassa was more terrified than ever as she found herself borne away in the dark hood; for now that she was in the power of the giants, how much more she had to dread than when with the gnomes! Her cries to be re-released were of no avail, but seemed only to have the effect of increasing the giant's speed, for he splashed through the ocean, and strode over hills, and jumped across valleys with such swiftness that in a very short time he stood before the high wall of rock that shut in the gnomes' domains. Then, carefully opening his hood, he picked Wassa out and placed her upon a tree in front of him, that he might keep one eye on her. Then he carefully took up the elf and held him before his eyes for a moment, to assure himself that this time no mistake had been made.

"Now, my fine prince, take us to thy royal sire, or rather bring him to us, as the dwarf's castle would be rather small for one of our size, and we will make the compact; but let us have a good look at thee, my pretty dwarf prince, ere we resign thee, for the features of thy race are so small it is hard for us to tell one from another."

So saying, Cloudcatcher placed the elf on the branch of an oak tree that grew near by.

The elf, as soon as he was released, executed a fantastic dance, and making a low obeisance, said: —

> "Sire, the prince, — or, if thou please,
> Toto the Slim, — I'm both of these.
> To Rondo quick his son now bring,
> And he will greet thee as his king."
> Then a grimace and a gay laugh
> And twirl of his beloved mustache,
> Or that part of his tiny face
> Which once had been the mustache's place,
> Toto the elf, with saucy bow,
> Said to the maid, as he bowed low,
> "Sorry to cause thee so much pain,
> But I will not offend again."

Then suddenly sliding down the tree, Toto

the Slim disappeared before the giant recovered from the surprise the elf's words had caused him.

When he fully realized the extent to which he had been duped, King Cloudcatcher flew into a great rage. His angry bellows reverberated among the hills and startled every living creature for miles about. The other giants hastened to the assistance of their king, and between his yells of rage they managed to understand the cause of the disturbance. The impulsive fellows quickly espoused the quarrel of their king.

"War to the dwarfs! Trample them to death! Batter down their gates!" cried the giants excitedly as they assembled in front of King Rondo's castle.

"Take thy club, Twigtwister, and batter against yon door!" cried the king. "And do thou, Rockroller, bring one of thy largest bowlders."

Selecting a massive oak that grew half way down the hill, Twigtwister, bending to the task, uprooted it and bore it to the top of the hill. At the same moment Rockroller appeared, bending beneath the weight of a gigantic rock that he had brought from the valley below.

Hastily stripping off the sturdy branches of the old oak as if they had been twigs, the giant

Twigtwister seized the topmost part of the tree securely in his huge right hand, and, swinging it about his head, brought it down with great force against the wall of rock.

THE LITTLE GRAY MAN'S DECISION.   235

The hill shook under the heavy blow, and in a moment Rockroller's huge rock came crashing against it with such violence that the earth shook and the wall gave way perceptibly.

"Ply thy club, Twigtwister, and do thou hurl another of thy bowlders," ordered the giant king. "A few more such blows and the dwarfs are ours."

Once more the giant Twigtwister's club battered against the rocky door, and again came Rockroller's stone against it, and with a loud report down came the rocky door, shattered to fragments. Within were seen a crowd of terrified gnomes huddled together, and at the sight of them the giants rent the air with shouts of victory.

"Twist their heads off! Toss them into yonder ocean!" cried the giants furiously as they made a rush for their victims.

"Stop! Stir not one foot!" cried a voice that caused the giants to stand as if rooted to the spot. With one accord they turned their eyes toward the voice, and beheld the little man in gray standing behind them on the crest of the hill.

The giants, a moment before so turbulent and ferocious, now stood like lambs before their master. Very stern was the countenance of the little man in gray as he looked at the great fellows with their powerful bodies and childish brains. For some time he regarded them in silence, then, with bent brows and uplifted finger, he spoke: —

"Is this the way ye keep the peace, ye great blundering fellows? Have ye so soon forgotten the compact?"

"Master," answered Cloudcatcher humbly, "we had sore grievance. A trick, a most dastardly trick, was played against us. The dwarf prince—"

"Enough!" cried the little gray man angrily. "Ye have shown that my gnomes and ye cannot dwell in peace together, therefore must ye part. Rondo, come hither," he added, beckoning to the gnome king, who at once approached and made a low obeisance. "Henceforth shalt thou keep well to thy domains within the hill. Extend thy realms as far underground as thou wilt, but seek not to attempt thy mischievous pranks above ground, else thou shalt forfeit thy fairy domains, and be banished to far-off lands. Come hither, friends," continued the little gray man, beckoning to the rover and his family, who, searching for the missing Wassa, had heard the tumult caused by the giants, and had ascended the hill to learn the cause of the commotion. "Come hither, friends, and harken to my words. Thou art well known to me. Thy daughter has been taught a lesson that she will not soon forget, and I command thee to keep at peace with thy neighbors. In future thou shalt have the right to fish only in the waters of yonder lake, and till the land that lies about it. No farther shalt thou go, neither shalt thou cast thy nets in any other waters. If thou shouldst disobey me, even that will be taken from thee, and thou must go to less pleasant lands.

"As for ye, my big and turbulent children," continued the little man in gray, addressing the giants once more, "ye are too dangerous when ye become angry, and ye must depart to yonder far-away mountains where ye will find nobody to injure. Now go, for the journey is a long one."

The giants dared not disobey the little man

in gray, and sorrowfully departed for what are now known as the Rocky Mountains. They were attached to the Blue Hill where they had lived for so many generations, and left it reluctantly. Ere they passed out of sight they paused to take a last look at the familiar line of hills, on which the rosy rays of the setting sun were falling,—a parting look at the "land of the After-glow." They sorrowfully watched the sun sink behind the trees, and as it disappeared the giant king gave expression to his regret in a stamp of his mighty foot that left its impression on the solid rock on which he stood; then they left the region forever.

The rock on which the giant stamped might have been seen, until within a few years, in the neighborhood of Blue Hill, where it was known as "The Devil's Rock." Many and many times have visitors climbed the huge bowlder to gaze at the impress of the giant's foot, half believing, as the tradition ran, that the king of evil himself had set his stamp there. The writer however, dear readers, has never had any faith in that story, for, if that had been the case, would not the print have taken the shape of a cloven foot? Much pleasanter is it to think of it as the footprint of the disappointed giant king, Cloudcatcher, as he left his old home.

The rover and his family obeyed the commands of the little man in gray, and so well did the arrangement work that the rover's and the hunter's families became fast friends, and in course of time cultivated much of the land in the vicinity of Blue Hill.

As for the gnomes, those busy sprites remained in their underground home, extending their domains and attending strictly to their own business.

The blue dragon-fly, after her imprisonment, lost much of her haughty demeanor, but her love of pleasure never left her, and has been transmitted to her descendants, who to this day may be seen sporting over the calm waters of the lakes that surround Blue Hill.

The brown beetle, too, lived a long and useful life, conscientiously doing his duty in his little world, and always retaining his admiration for the beautiful blue dragon-fly.

As for the elves, it seems as if the harmless, gay little creatures must be still in their old homes, for there are some people who think they have caught glimpses of them dancing around the fairy spring that to this day remains on Blue Hill, and these same people have often seen what looked very like the roguish face of Toto the Slim, downy mustache and all, looking out of the wild flowers.

One thing is certain, the "land of the Afterglow" still remains. Its rosy light glows long after the sun has sunk behind the western woods; but whether the little man in gray still makes this region his home is a doubtful point. The writer has sometimes thought she saw him vanishing in his sudden way as she came upon him, but very sensible people have told her it was a freak of her imagination, and very likely they were right; but she is *sure* that she has often seen — no, on second thought she will not say *what* she has seen, for you, too, dear readers, might think she imagined it, and that would grieve her sorely.

www.ingramcontent.com/pod-product-compliance
Lightning Source LLC
Chambersburg PA
CBHW020801230426
43666CB00007B/802